THE
KOALA
BOOK

ANN SHARP

PELICAN PUBLISHING COMPANY
Gretna 1995

To all the wild koalas

Published simultaneously in September 1995 by
    Pelican Publishing Company, Inc., in North America
    David Bateman Ltd. in New Zealand

Library of Congress Cataloging-in-Publication Data

Sharp, Ann, 1965-
    The koala book / Ann Sharp.
        p.   cm.
    Includes bibliographical references (p.   ) and index.
    ISBN 1-56554-160-X (hc)
    1. Koala.   2. Koala—Pictorial works.   I. Title.
QL737.M384S48 1995
599.2—dc20   95-32198
                                                                    CIP

Printed and bound in Hong Kong
Published by Pelican Publishing Company, Inc.
1101 Monroe Street, Gretna, Louisiana 70053

CONTENTS

ACKNOWLEDGEMENTS 8

INTRODUCTION — EVOLUTION 13

PHYSICAL ATTRIBUTES 29

NATIONAL DISTRIBUTION OF THE KOALA 49

THE LIFE OF THE KOALA 67

SOCIALISATION 83

KOALAS AND PEOPLE 99

HOT SPOTS 113

SYMBOLS OF THE KOALA 125

WHAT IS BEING DONE? 139

BIBLIOGRAPHY 156

PICTURE CREDITS 158

INDEX 159

Acknowledgements

Koalas have lent inspiration to this book, but their relationship with people, and vice versa, made it a reality. Scientific papers and general articles written about the koala provide explanations of various aspects of its biology, but there is also much to be gained from the quiet contemplation of individual koalas. Thanks to all those koalas who have been observed over the years.

Now to people; thank you one and all: Debbie Tabart, who had the confidence to force my transformation from couch potato to first-time author; my Mum, Joan Sharp, my most revered editor; Steve Phillips, a person whose love of the bush and gentle, compassionate regard for koalas and other wildlife is contagious; Christiane Scheffler, without whom the selection of illustrations would have been more of a nightmare, and whose calming influence and love of photography and Australia taught me a lot; Philip Wright, a freelance photographer who enthusiastically and selflessly offered his help to the Australian Koala Foundation; John Garnsworthy, for wonderful diagrams and ongoing laughter; Georgeanne Irvine and Ron Garrison, both very generous San Diego Zoo koala-loving photographers; John Callaghan and his red pen; the many koala researchers listed in the bibliography; Wendy Blanshard, Paul O'Callaghan and Jackie from the Lone Pine Koala Sanctuary; Ray Chafer of Dreamworld's Koala Country; koala keepers and carers around the world; John Stark and Wendy Hollier for wonderful words of encouragement; Sean Leahy and Gerard Piper for allowing me to rifle through their cartoon files; Dad for lifelong encouragement; Jenny, John and Lauren Sando for use (and help with) the computer; Anne Shaw and Joanne Johnston for allowing photographers into their home; the children and teachers of Chatswood Hills Primary School; Jo Knights for always lending her camera; Lorraine and Jane, Monica, Danni and Linda, and everyone at the Australian Koala Foundation; Tracey Borgfeldt and Paul Bateman, my publishers, for their encouragement and help.

INTRODUCTION – EVOLUTION

Above: A young koala nestled in its mother's fur looks out innocently upon the world. The koala's great popularity has much to do with its appealing face.

Opposite: Where once the koala relied upon the eucalypts for its survival, its future now depends on people.

Koalas, like the other animals and plants native to Australia, have spent a long, long time separated from the rest of the world — on a life raft as it were — evolving in isolation for roughly 45 million years. This isolation has meant that Australia's wildlife is perceived to be different in the wider world view, possessing an exotic quality that translates into something of fascination for people all over the world. The koala, more than any other animal, has become the living icon of Australia.

Good looks and a gentle disposition have served to elevate an animal unique in the world from an anonymous life amongst the eucalypts to international fame. The koala enjoys great popularity but at the same time finds itself facing severe threats from human influence. It is a paradox that people so enamoured with an animal like the koala can contribute so dramatically to its demise. Where once the koala simply relied upon eucalypt forests for its survival, its fate now depends upon the decisions made by the human race.

The better we understand the koala and its surrounding environment, the better equipped we will be to make decisions which will contribute to its long-term conservation. While its part in the complex web of life on the planet is admittedly small, the koala's positive image has the ability to encourage and attract many people to understand the intricacy, fragility and interdependence of all life on Earth.

Welcome to the koala's world...

The evolution of Australia

Australia was not always a separate isolated continent. It was once part of a supercontinent called Gondwana which existed during the Mesozoic era, between 245 and 65 million years ago. There was also a time when all landmasses on Earth were joined into one enormous continent called Pangaea, from which Gondwana split. When this separation occurred, each landmass took with it the building blocks of life, and as time passed and geographic and climatic conditions changed, lifeforms adapted to survive.

Due to the inexorable movement of the Earth's tectonic plates, continents are constantly moving, albeit slowly. When Gondwana began to break up towards the end of the Mesozoic era, the dinosaurs were coming to the end of their reign and the first marsupials had appeared. Each part of Gondwana carried the possibility of a koala with it; that is, koalas potentially could have evolved in South America, Antarctica, New Zealand, Papua New Guinea, India, Madagascar or Africa, but they did not. Only Australia produced the specific conditions to prompt the evolution of the koala. There is a profound message in this uniqueness and it applies to every living thing on Earth.

Below: The edge of a vast continent — The Twelve Apostles near Port Campbell, Victoria, on Australia's southern coast.

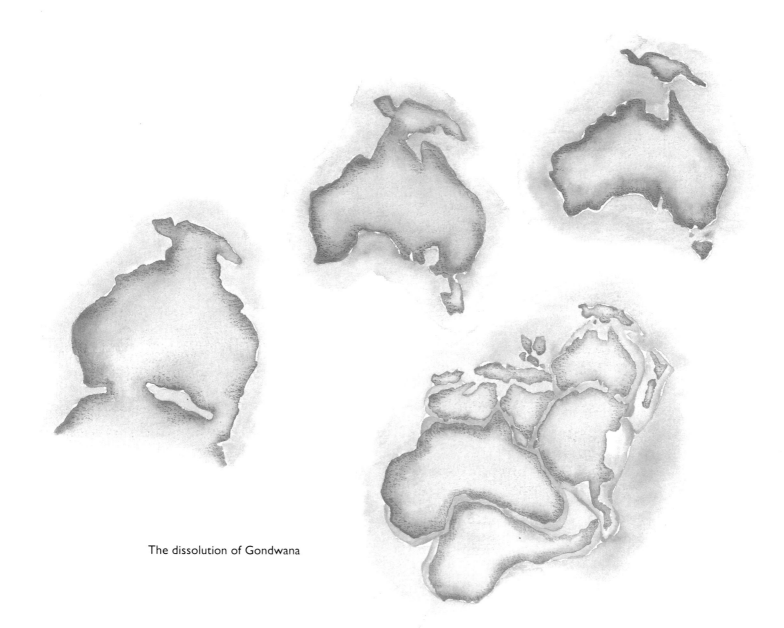

The dissolution of Gondwana

The dissolution of Gondwana was complete when Australia finally broke away from Antarctica approximately 45 million years ago and began its long period of isolation. Fossil remains of marsupials have been found in most countries that once formed part of Gondwana but living specimens occur only in North and South America, Australia, Papua New Guinea and some of its surrounding islands.

Isolation from the other continents and the lack of competition from placental mammals provided an opportunity for the marsupials to dominate and fill the available niches in Australia. The changing climate and the adaptation of vegetation to survive in the increasingly arid conditions played a major part in the diversification of Australia's marsupials. They have split into a fascinating array of animals which occupy many and varied environments and niches. Today, marsupials can be found in rainforests and deserts, underground or in the trees; some move quickly, some move slowly. Approximately two-thirds of all the living marsupials are found in Australia and Papua New Guinea.

Marsupials are one of three classifications of mammals, the warm-blooded vertebrates. The others are the monotremes and the placentals. Fossil evidence shows that mammals evolved from reptiles and their differentiating characteristics are that mammals are warm-blooded, they all have hair or fur and they feed their young on milk.

The main differences between the three mammalian sub-groups are their reproductive systems. Monotremes lay eggs, marsupials give birth to their young at an embryonic stage of development and placentals give birth to well-formed young. Formerly, it was believed that the marsupials represented an intermediate evolutionary step between the monotremes and placentals but now it is understood that the three evolved separately. Marsupials exhibit a wide range of highly specialised adaptations to survive in many different environments, and although the word marsupial originates from the Latin *marsupium*, meaning pouch, not all marsupials have pouches. Some female marsupials form temporary pouches or skin folds over the teat where the young are suckled and some have no pouch at all.

There are two major groupings within the marsupial family: the carnivorous marsupials, including South American opossums, predatory Australian marsupials and omnivorous bandicoots; and the herbivorous marsupials, including possums, kangaroos, koalas and wombats.

Above left: The koala's ancestors exchanged life on the ground for life in the trees some 25 million years ago.

Above top right: The wombat is considered to be the closest relative of the koala within the marsupial group.

Above bottom right: A brushtail possum peeps out at the world. Like many Australian marsupials, possums are nocturnal.

Scientific classification is still developing and there is some question as to where exactly some species fit within the currently accepted groupings. According to traditional classification based on dentition (tooth configuration and design), the marsupials fall into two basic orders; the Polyprotodonta (meaning 'many front teeth') which are basically carnivorous or omnivorous, and the Diprotodonta (meaning 'two front teeth') which are basically herbivorous.

Koalas belong to the Diprotodonta and like the other members of that group they have one pair of strongly developed incisors on their lower jaw. The fusing of the second and third toes on their hindfeet is another feature that confirms their membership of this order.

Within the Diprotodonta order, koalas and wombats are grouped together into a further sub-group or superfamily called Vombatoidea and wombats are generally agreed to be the koala's closest living relative, although there is still some doubt.

The koala has its own family classification called Phascolarctidae, of which it is the only living representative. Fossilised remains of several extinct members of the koala family have been found, dating back as far as 25 million years. While fossilised evidence of the koala's ancestors is rare, consisting mainly of teeth and jaw fragments, it suggests that three different genera (*Perikoala*, *Madakoala* and *Litokoala*) were all tree-

dwelling folivores (eaters of foliage as distinct from eaters of grasses, i.e., herbivores) and were not dissimilar to today's koala, *Phascolarctos cinereus*.

Australia was not always the arid 'sunburnt' country it is today. It was once covered with rainforest and it was here that the koala's ancestors lived. The interesting thing about the fossil record is that traces of ancestral koalas are very rare. A reasonable explanation seems to be that ancient koalas themselves were rare, perhaps because they specialised in feeding on the ancestors of today's *Eucalyptus* trees, which were sparsely distributed within rainforests.

As Australia began to 'dry out', due to the combined effects of an ice age which froze much of the Earth's circulating water into icecaps and Australia's slow movement closer to the Equator, the genus *Eucalyptus* came to dominate the continent's open forests and woodlands as the range of rainforest receded. Koalas, specialising on eucalypts, were well placed from an evolutionary point of view and it seems that the two species have been evolving together for many millions of years. It also seems that today koalas are more abundant and widely distributed than their ancestors would have been, although human impact on the forest of Australia is rapidly reducing that advantage.

The Aboriginal people reached Australia 60,000 years ago or more and their legends from the Dreaming (the Aboriginal oral history) describe the creation of Australia. Aboriginal creation legends all describe a creator power or great spirit which brought the landscape and climate into being, then the plants and animals and finally the people. The progression of events described in these creation legends, from the gradual forming of land and climate, evolution of plants and animals and finally the arrival of *Homo sapiens*, correlates chronologically with modern scientific understanding of the evolution of the Australian continent and the lifeforms it supports.

Above: McKenzie Falls, Grampians, The Gariwerd National Park. Ancestral koalas once survived in the rainforest, but today's koala no longer occupies this niche.

Opposite top: Aboriginal creation legends describe a creator power or great spirit which brought the landscape into being.

Opposite bottom: Danny Eastwood, an aboriginal artist whose totem is the koala, made this mural on Australia Day 1991. He says, "The hands from every caring person in this world are needed to protect the koala on his future survival journey."

Left: A lone tree in a field where once there would have been a forest. European settlers transformed the landscape, disregarding the needs of Australia's native animals.

Delicate flowers (far left and middle left) grace the Australian bush, along with the more hardy xanthorrhoeas (left), which are designed for harsh conditions.

Opposite: Of more than pure aesthetic value, eucalypts provide homes for koalas, possums, gliders, snakes, bats and birds.

Left: Australia is a vast continent of widely contrasting environments and infinite beauty.

There are various Dreaming legends about the koala which explain its physical peculiarities — the absence of a tail, the extremely long intestine and the strength of its shoulders and arms. Legends vary between regions but there is one repeated in several areas which warns that if people do not pay respect to traditions associated with the koala, it will bring on a great drought.

'Koala' is commonly thought to mean 'no drink' in the Aboriginal language, despite the fact that there are many different languages spoken by Aboriginal people throughout the country. Koala is the name that became widely accepted, although early written accounts by white settlers, reflecting the diversity of Aboriginal dialects/languages, describe it with names as diverse as cullewine, koolewong, colo, colah, koolah, kaola, koala, karbor, boorabee and goribun.

Its established scientific name is *Phascolarctos cinereus*, which literally means 'ash-grey pouched bear' and until quite recently koalas were commonly referred to as 'koala bears'. Koalas may resemble teddy bears but the comparison ends there. Koalas are not bears, they are marsupials, although their scientific name will continue to confuse as it is almost impossible to change.

In the two hundred plus short years since white settlement of Australia, human impact on the wild koala population has been severe and drastic. The food and shelter resources that were available to the koala prior to 1788 have been reduced by roughly four-fifths. All the forests in Australia at that time could be considered 'old growth'. Today less than three percent of the old growth forests remain, and these are still under pressure to be logged for timber and woodchips.

Koalas share their environment with some of Australia's most well known birds. Opposite are (clockwise from top left): scaly-breasted lorikeets, which rely on hollow trees for nesting sites; a kookaburra; galahs catching the last rays of the setting sun; and a pelican.

Left: An eastern water dragon, silent and camouflaged amongst the leaf litter.

Queensland

New
South
Wales

South Australia

Victoria

Left: Queensland, New South
Wales, Victoria and South
Australia are the only states in
Australia where koalas are
found in the wild.

Most Australians have never seen an old growth tree, as the coastal forests observed by most of us are 'regrowth' forest comprising eucalypts of no more than fifty years of age. It is difficult to picture what Australia would have looked like when the First Fleet sailed into Botany Bay, but it must have been magnificent.

The majesty of a eucalypt over four hundred years old is breathtaking to behold and it can take up to fifteen people to embrace the girth of some ancient surviving eucalypts. While we can appreciate imposing old eucalypts for their aesthetic beauty, a wide variety of native animals relies on such old trees for shelter. It takes from two to three hundred years for a eucalypt to form nesting hollows which provide the homes for possums, gliders, bats, snakes and birds, including every single variety of the beautiful parrots (including galahs, budgerigars and cockatoos) that Australia is so famous for. Australia's remaining old growth forests teem with life where many coastal forests are growing silent as the animals disappear because of too much disturbance.

The first white settlers understood very little about the unique flora and fauna of Australia. The forests were viewed as a spectacular timber resource and the animals' dependence on the forest ecosystems was largely overlooked. Attitudes have changed greatly since then and an increasing number of people appreciate the natural world. However, it is much harder now to restore the wealth of nature that has been destroyed than it would have been to treasure and protect what we had.

Koalas are becoming well known as a species suffering the detrimental effects caused by the human population, yet they are only one small example of the many plants and animals unique to Australia that are disappearing before our eyes.

Left: Queensland, New South Wales, Victoria and South Australia are the only states in Australia where koalas are found in the wild.

Opposite top: The Brisbane city skyline at night. City burghers like to claim Brisbane as the koala capital of the world, but expansion of the city's suburbs is destroying hope of the koala's future survival.

Opposite bottom: Millions of hectares of Australia's native forests have been cleared to make way for human endeavour. Agricultural lands given over to sheep do not make safe havens for koalas.

Following pages: To the untrained eye these views of "Man from Snowy River" country have a certain pastoral beauty, but they are severely modified landscapes in which many native animals struggle to survive.

PHYSICAL ATTRIBUTES

During its evolutionary history, the koala has adapted to a slowly changing landscape and climate. Its ability to live on a diet extremely low in nutritional value illustrates the amazing ability of nature to produce life in the face of adversity. While science has not yet answered all the conundrums posed by the koala's physical characteristics, we can be sure they are there for a reason. Whether they are remnants of some ancestral form or adaptations for life in the trees, the koala's physical characteristics set it apart from all other species; it is unique.

What does a koala look like?

Koalas have faces that mesmerise the human observer, and their gentle expressions and soft fur belie the fact that they are wiry, muscular, strong animals that can easily scale a 30-metre gumtree. They are arboreal, meaning they live in trees, and their bodies are adapted accordingly. Unlike other Australian tree-dwelling marsupials, they do not have

Above and top right: The koala's well-developed claws allow it to grip firmly onto trees when it climbs.

Bottom right: A koala's hind paw: with its clawless 'thumb' or big toe; first and second toes fused to form the perfect grooming tool; and strong, sharp, curved claws to aid climbing.

Opposite: A solid mass in the treetops, an outstretched paw and the rough outline of an ear are indicators to an observer on the ground that a koala sits in this tree.

an obvious tail to assist with balance, agility and climbing. However, other characteristics, such as their slow metabolism and strategy of conserving energy with long periods of rest, make tail-assisted acrobatics unnecessary.

Koalas have big ears and a prominent nose, indicators that hearing and a sense of smell are important to them, and their arms, legs, paws and claws assist climbing and grasping tree branches. When viewed from the ground, the koala's bottom has a speckled or cloud-like appearance which acts as a type of camouflage. If you are looking for koalas in the wild, they are often elusive. Their fur merges with the colour of the bark and they can appear to be part of the tree they are sitting in. If nestled amongst the topmost leafy branches, a koala will be almost impossible to detect. Individual personality can determine whether a koala will try to remain unseen by human observers. Some are extremely shy, some are nonchalant and one or two display gregarious behaviour. Most of all, they are gentle.

People usually first see koalas in a sanctuary or zoo but nothing compares to the joy of seeing one in the wild where it belongs. Nothing is more rewarding than finding a well-hidden koala in a eucalypt tree, a fluffy ear or outstretched paw disclosing its presence. You can get close to sanctuary animals, touch them, look them in the eye and they are

Left: The large nose, the fluffy ears, the appealing gaze — the composition of its facial features is largely responsible for the koala's popularity.

Below left: Hearing is an important sense for the koala, and its large ears capture the many sounds of the bush.

Opposite top: The scent gland in the middle of a male koala's chest produces secretions used for marking out territory. It becomes more prominent during the breeding season and as males grow older.

Opposite bottom: A male koala marking the base of a tree to communicate territoriality to other koalas.

infinitely appealing and heart-warming. However, to see a wild koala is to begin to understand its world. It is as much a part of the tree as a whale is part of the ocean. Remove it from its natural surroundings and something is lost.

How does it interpret its environment?

The koala has a large head relative to its body size and the composition of its facial features is largely responsible for the popularity it enjoys today. The brain is relatively small which has led to speculation that the koala has very low intelligence. This claim has not been substantiated and some believe it to be yet another unfair myth created around an animal seemingly devoid of grace, slow of movement and of soporific habit.

Because it is a mostly nocturnal animal, hearing is an important sense to the koala and its ears are relatively large to catch sounds in the bush. Ears vary between individuals but generally have a 'fluffy' appearance.

The koala's eyes have a vertically slit iris similar to a cat's eyes. The pupil dilates at night, when the koala is most active, to allow in maximum light. Generally the koala's eyesight is poor and it depends more upon its senses of smell and hearing to interpret the surrounding environment.

Its most prominent facial feature, the large nose, is possibly the most complex part of its anatomy. It is covered with soft, dark, leathery skin, similar to that covering the palms and soles of the feet and is an extremely sensitive organ. The koala relies on its sense of smell for selecting its food, sensing danger and perceiving the presence of other koalas. Their sense of smell can indicate to males when females are in oestrus and therefore ready to mate. It also tells koalas about territoriality and the boundaries of each individual's home range, which trees are meeting places and which are out of bounds. The size of the nose hints at the complexity of the koala's olfactory system and its importance to the koala's survival.

The scent gland on the male koala's chest is used to mark trees, signalling territorial ownership to other koalas. This behaviour reduces the need for confrontation between individuals, effectively minimising the need to waste precious energy fighting. Male koalas try to avoid one another, although fighting will occur over territorial disputes. Females will also fight other females, or the unwanted advances of males. Koalas will defend themselves against attack or capture using their powerful claws and teeth. Although koalas can inflict some painful wounds they can generally be overcome by humans and dogs.

Features that distinguish male from female

The visual differences between males and females include the presence of a scrotum and chest scent gland in males and a pouch in females, but when viewing a koala high in a tree from the ground, it is difficult to distinguish such differences. Female koalas tend to be 'prettier' than males thanks to their facial features and smaller size: fully grown males can be up to fifty percent larger than adult females and the male's head shape is slightly different, with a Roman-style bump above the nose.

Identifying the sex of a koala from size and facial features alone, however, does not always work because sub-adult koalas, say from nine months to eighteen months of age, all have the wide-eyed innocence and beauty of youth. Adolescent males can be similar in size to fully grown females.

Males and females reach sexual maturity around two years of age, but do not usually become sexually active for another year or two. Young male koalas are subordinate to older males, who occupy home ranges closest to breeding females, and they defer to authority until they reach their full size and maturity. Usually males do not mate until they are about four years of age, when their position in the social hierarchy is higher. Females have been recorded producing their first young around two years of age, but each individual is different and they are more often first-time mothers at three or four years.

Body size and proportion of the fully grown koala varies with age, sex, nutrition and geography. Koalas living in colder climates, say Victoria, are generally larger and their fur darker and thicker than those living in warmer climates, say Queensland. It seems there are exceptions to every rule and some Victorian koalas are light in colour while some Queenslanders are dark. Generally though, the koalas appear to have adapted for climate and temperature, a long, dark-coloured fur providing more insulation than a short light-coloured one.

A fully grown dominant male koala in Victoria can weigh up to 14 kilograms and a Victorian female up to 11 kilograms, although the average weight is lower; 12 kilograms for males and 8 kilograms for females. Queensland koalas are generally smaller and, on average, males weigh around 8 kilograms and females weigh around 6 kilograms. A koala living in a district with lower average rainfall and poorer soils will tend to be smaller than one living in a more fertile environment.

The koala is one of the largest arboreal marsupials in Australia, being slightly smaller than the tree kangaroo. If it were much bigger it would risk regular falls from the trees and thinner leaf-bearing branches would be unable to sustain its weight. Its diet contains very little nutrition and requires a complex digestion. Koalas are large enough to contain a digestive system capable of processing the quantity of leaves they need to ingest and small enough for those leaves to provide adequate energy.

Eucalyptus, or 'gum', leaves from a variety of eucalypt species are the koala's staple diet.

Adaptations for a eucalyptus diet

Koalas feed preferentially on the leaves of the genus *Eucalyptus* although they supplement their diet with other species such as *Acacia*, *Melaleuca* and *Allocasuarina*. Eucalyptus leaves are very fibrous and low in nutrition, and to most animals they are extremely poisonous, but they are the koala's staple diet.

To cope with a diet low in nutritional value and high in toxicity, nature has equipped koalas with specialised adaptations. A very slow metabolic rate allows koalas to retain food within their digestive system for a relatively long period of time, effectively maximising the amount of energy able to be extracted. Simultaneously, this slow metabolic rate minimises energy requirements. A koala's daily energy needs are comparatively lower than other herbivores and allow it to survive on a diet composed predominantly of eucalyptus leaves.

In addition to its ability to extract the maximum goodness from eucalyptus leaves, the digestive system detoxifies those chemicals within the leaves that are poisonous. Very few animals are able to ingest eucalyptus leaves without becoming sick; koalas, greater gliders and ringtail possums are the only mammals able to digest them.

A eucalypt leaf is composed largely of fibrous cell walls, essential oils and phenolics, which provide very little energy and which can interfere with the digestive process. Phenolics and toxic compounds are produced by the eucalyptus tree as a protective mechanism to deter leaf eaters like insects and koalas. The avoidance of most eucalypt species by koalas may indicate an intolerable level of leaf toxicity. Of those tree species used by koalas (very roughly seventy eucalypt and thirty non-eucalypt species nationally, although a very much lower figure at a local level, say five to ten, the primary browse trees being eucalypts), koalas will avoid some and use others of the same species, indicating that there are factors additional to tree species which make leaves palatable to them. It seems there is a threshold level of toxicity in eucalyptus foliage beyond which koalas cannot or will not cope. If a tree is growing

Right: Koalas' teeth are specialised tools designed to deal with the very fibrous leaves of eucalyptus trees. Top and bottom incisors nip leaves from the tree, then the molars grind them to a fine pulp before they are swallowed.

Opposite: Koalas are extremely fastidious in their choice of leaves; each handful is sniffed very carefully before a bite is taken.

in good conditions, it does not produce as much toxic defence as a tree growing in harsh conditions. Rich soils, rainfall, water table and drainage appear to affect positively the nutritional composition of eucalypt leaves and the probability of the presence of koalas.

Koalas extract energy from eucalyptus foliage in the form of sugars, starch, lipids and protein. Then the remaining dietary fibre, made up of the cell walls, goes through a long process of digestion where any remaining nutrients and energy are extracted. Water from the leaves is also absorbed with minimal wastage in the faeces and urine.

Koalas are extremely fastidious in their choice of leaves. They extend an arm and select a handful which is sniffed very carefully before a bite is taken. Leaves are nipped from the branch with careful precision before being chewed to a fine pulp and swallowed.

The koala's teeth are specialised to deal with its particular diet. The front incisors top and bottom nip the leaves from the tree. A gap between the incisors and the molars, called a 'diastema', allows the tongue to move the mass of leaves around the mouth efficiently without being bitten. Molars are shaped to enable the koala to cut and shear the leaves rather than just to crush them. This means that in addition to extracting moisture from the leaves, the koala's teeth tear cell walls apart, releasing more absorbable energy.

Most notable in its digestive system is the caecum, a 200-cm long and 10-cm in diameter tube which comes off at a tangent from the main digestive tract leading to the rectum. A mechanism within the digestive system separates the leaf matter into two categories of fine and coarse. The finer leaf matter is diverted into the caecum where it is retained for further digestion.

Like a number of other herbivorous mammals, koalas have formed a symbiotic relationship with micro-organisms which live in their caecum and assist with the breakdown of the leaves. These micro-organisms perform a function similar to enzymes. A type of fermentation occurs in the caecum, but contrary to popular myth this does not contribute to 'drunkenness' often attributed to the koala. Its sleepy state is due to a slow metabolic rate, an adaptation for tackling a diet low in nutrition and for conserving energy.

Scientific tests have found the amount of additional energy drained from the leaf matter retained in the caecum is proportionately insignificant from a digestive point of view. This suggests the caecum has some other function. It could also act as a mechanism for absorbing water or for accessing additional nitrogen and protein locked in the cell walls, but this is yet to be proven.

Unwanted toxins are expelled in the faeces and urine and some of the essential oil is probably used in the male's scent gland.

Koalas consume 200–400 grams of leaves per day. Many are rejected after the smell test or dislodged during the selection process, and a telltale sign of a koala's presence in the wild is the presence of newly broken off twigs and leaves at the base of the tree.

The majority of water ingested by koalas comes from eucalyptus leaves, though some additional water is found as dew or rain droplets. Drought conditions reduce the koala's access to water and can severely affect wild populations. They have been reported descending to the base of trees to drink water left by children in outback districts during dry periods.

Koalas have also been observed eating bark, gumnuts and soil. Soil provides additional minerals for the diet, but it is ingested only occasionally.

Above: Faecal pellets resemble olive pips and are often difficult to locate amongst leaf litter. They are dry and fibrous, and, when fresh, retain a faint and pleasant smell of eucalyptus.

Opposite: Koalas are strong climbers. They have short, stocky bodies that are lean and muscular, but comparatively long, strong limbs that can easily support their weight when climbing.

Adaptations for an arboreal lifestyle

Koalas spend most of their lives among the limbs and leaves of eucalyptus trees; theirs is an arboreal lifestyle.

Unlike other arboreal marsupials like possums and gliders, koalas do not seem to require the acrobatic agility or quickness of movement aided by a tail because they are large enough not to fear predators in the tree tops, and they do not have to hunt a moving prey. In addition, their need to conserve energy means they rest motionless for much of the time.

Koalas are strong climbers and their bodies are lean and muscular, a characteristic often overlooked because of their soft ears and furry faces.

These are both classic koala poses. One picture (opposite) shows a koala during hot weather, and the animal is doing its best to get cool. The other shot (right) was taken on a cooler day, when the two koalas are curled into balls, reducing the area of their bodies exposed to the wind.

They have short stocky bodies but comparatively long, strong limbs which support their weight when climbing. Their hands, feet and claws are perfectly adapted to grasping and clinging to branches and their balance is excellent.

When approaching a tree to climb, koalas spring from the ground and catch their front claws in the bark, then bound upwards with apparent ease, both hands then both feet. Observing koala trees in the bush one can often see where the front claws first dug into the bark and slid through it with the exertion of the animal pushing off to climb further upwards. Koalas always climb up and down the trunks of trees with head uppermost, which means they descend bottom first. Coming down is a slower more careful process, one leg placed at a time.

A koala's instinct is to climb and find safety in the branches of a gumtree. When faced with suburban settings, they will climb walls, fences, lightpoles, street signs and have been known to outwit the designers of so-called 'koala-proof' fences. While their appearance out of context has a comical quality, such sights demonstrate the tragedy of the destruction of their natural environment.

The strength of their limbs is augmented by the design of their hands and feet. They have long, curved, powerful claws and of the five clawed digits on their hands, two are opposed like 'thumbs', allowing for a firmer grip. Their hind feet have one clawless 'thumb' and the second and third toes are fused together, forming the ideal grooming tool. Ticks are removed with the fused claws and while they do suffer from ticks, a healthy koala can generally keep itself relatively free of them. Debilitated and sick koalas have more difficulty, possibly because their energy reserves are too low even for simple grooming. Koala carers report that when they receive a sick koala for care, it often has an unusually high number of ticks.

Koalas regularly descend to the ground to change trees. It is on the ground that they are most vulnerable. They walk with a seemingly awkward gait, front right foot then back left foot, front left foot, back right foot and so on. They can also run, and when they do they adopt a different locomotion, both front, then both back feet, as when they are climbing the trunk of a tree.

Some koalas spend longer on the ground than others, depending on the size of their home range and the distances between trees. Koalas living near human habitation often have to travel further on the ground than koalas in an undisturbed environment and face more hazards, such as dogs, motor vehicles and swimming pools, and obstacles, such as fences.

Koalas have been observed swimming, although this is not a regular occurrence unless made necessary by the location of a particular animal's home range. They have been known to swim rivers swollen by

Below: A koala's claws slide down the bark as it climbs, indicating the exertion required to ascend the tree.

flood and early this century there were reports of koalas swimming the Pittwater (a large body of water at the entrance of the Hawkesbury River just north of Sydney) to arrive on Scotland Island, a distance of at least 2 kilometres. Koalas in suburbia sometimes drown in backyard swimming pools, not because they can't swim but because they cannot get out. Residents in koala areas are encouraged to instal special ropes trailing into their swimming pools to solve this problem.

In the safety and comfort of their home trees, koalas assume a wide variety of sitting and sleeping postures depending upon available tree forks, the weather conditions and the time of day. In the bush, the moods of the day vary with the passing hours and koalas will move around the tree to find the most comfortable spot, perhaps in the sun, out of the sun, in a position to catch the breezes or somewhere to shelter from the wind and rain. To a koala, a tree is not just a tree. It is a large house with different spaces for different times.

Some branches appear to be custom-made for a koala to recline on, others look just a touch too small or narrow, yet on these a koala can rest comfortably for hours. Tree forks provide safe places to sleep, and koalas will wedge themselves between branches so as not to fall. You can see them curled up, football-shaped or sprawled out, legs hanging down. In cold, wet and windy weather koalas are most likely to curl themselves up into a ball to reduce surface area exposed and retain maximum warmth. On hot dry or humid days, koalas arrange themselves in 'open' positions most conducive to keeping cool. The fur on their chests is light in colour enabling it to reflect heat; it is also longer

Below left: Koalas are at their most vulnerable on the ground.

Below right: This koala must be sick or debilitated in some way because its fur should not be 'wet', even after a downpour of rain. The fur of healthy koalas will never appear to be 'wet'.

Right: The fur on a koala's bottom is particularly dense, to provide cushioning against the hard and angular branches.

Opposite: The koala's fur — short, soft, springy to the touch — is very densely packed and has one of the highest insulative properties of any animal in the world.

than the fur on their backs, assisting with ventilation when a breeze brushes by. The koala's postural strategy to regulate heat is one of the characteristics that endears it most to people. A koala fast asleep with its legs and arms dangling is a sight few of us can pass without a smile.

From a human point of view, sitting for hours in the fork of a tree would be extremely uncomfortable but to koalas it is a way of life. The fur on a koala's bottom is densely packed to provide cushioning for the hard and angular branches upon which it positions itself.

Sleeping and resting during the day are extremely important adaptations for the koala to conserve energy. Koalas are nocturnal animals, most active during the night and at dawn and dusk, because during these cooler hours they are less likely to lose precious moisture and energy from the exertion of activity than they would during the heat of the day.

For each day in a koala's life, an average of eighteen to twenty-one hours are spent resting, between one to two hours are allocated to feeding, about the same to moving either around the tree or between trees, and roughly fifteen minutes remains for grooming and another fifteen minutes for social interaction.

Adaptations for climate

The koala's fur is considered to have one of the highest insulative properties of any animal in the world, comparable to mammals living in polar regions. This is one reason it was in such high demand during the 1800s and early 1900s for the international fur trade. Over most of its body, the fur is short, densely packed, very soft and springy to the touch. It varies in colour between individuals and environments from light grey, through darker greys to brown. When female koalas carry back-young, their fur is worn thin by the youngsters clambering claws and an otherwise grey back can appear brownish through wear and tear.

Since koalas do not seek shelter in hollows or build nests, their fur must provide protection from the elements. When it rains, the water runs off the koala's fur, much like water off a duck's back. Only koalas that are sick or debilitated in some way will appear to be 'wet'. Compare a wild koala who lives exposed to the elements with a captive koala, sheltered by roofed enclosures and you will notice the wild animal's fur looks more weathered.

Communication

Koalas employ a range of vocalisations to communicate with one another over relatively large distances. In the male repertoire there is a deep grunting bellow which is used to communicate both its physical and its social position. It can sound like a far-off rumbling, like a motorbike starting up or like a pig snorting. Males save fighting energy by bellowing about their dominance. Bellowing is also prevalent during the breeding season and allows other animals to locate and accurately pinpoint the position of the caller.

Female koalas do not bellow as often as males, but their calls too are used to communicate aggression as well as being part of sexual behaviour. Watching and listening to koalas coming together to mate, the casual observer could get the impression they were witnessing a fight. To the uninitiated, the koala's vocal repertoire comes as a surprise because it does not match the popular cute and cuddly image.

Both males and females share one common call that is elicited by fear. It is a sickening cry like a baby screaming, and is made by animals under stress. It is often accompanied by shaking.

Mothers and babies make soft clicking, squeaking sounds to one another as well as gentle grunts to signal displeasure or annoyance. A gentle humming or murmuring sound is another type of vocalisation.

In the middle of the bush, a koala will contribute to the communication between other species. An owl calls, another responds and following a slight pause, a male koala begins to bellow, adding his piece to the composition of night sounds.

A wild, wise and weather-beaten koala endures a winter wind, insulated and warm thanks to its thick coat.

NATIONAL DISTRIBUTION OF THE KOALA

Opposite and above: The distribution of koalas is dependent upon the existence of suitable habitat: trees are their lifeblood.

General distribution

Koala populations are patchily distributed within remaining areas of suitable habitat in eastern and south-eastern Australia. The northern extremity of their range is the Atherton Tablelands west of Cairns and the southern extremity is coastal Victoria. Koalas occur in the wild in Queensland, New South Wales, Victoria and South Australia. The density of individual populations depends largely on the quality and size of available habitat. While koalas can still be found in many parts of their former range, the habitat available to them has been reduced greatly since white settlement of Australia. This has resulted in drastic reduction and fragmentation of the national koala population.

It is difficult to define accurately the range and size of koala populations prior to white settlement because of a number of 'unknowns'. Firstly, there is a shortage of documentation about koalas in historical

and anecdotal records from the early years of settlement. This could mean that early settlers did not notice or record sightings of koalas, or that koalas were not present in large numbers where early settlement occurred. Secondly, it is assumed that owing to the expansion of white settlement, Aboriginal people and dingoes, which constituted the koala's main predators, were removed from many of their traditional hunting lands and, as a consequence, the koala population increased until koalas were reported to be abundant. Stories passed down from the 1800s tell of koalas too numerous to count and of koalas venturing into the houses on rural properties and making a 'nuisance' of themselves. On the one hand this could be explained by a population explosion, but on the other it could have been that large numbers of koalas had been displaced by massive clearing of the eucalypts that sustained them.

At the time of white settlement, eucalypt forests covered much of the east coast and they provided a large habitat resource for koalas. While today's understanding of the koala's habitat selection and ranging behaviour tells us that they would not have been evenly distributed throughout this range, their potential distribution would have been far greater then than it is today, notwithstanding the influence of aboriginal hunting pressure.

Above: Trees growing along watercourses often provide the best habitat for koalas.

Above: This historical photograph shows the land after the timber and scrub have been felled and burnt. Note the large size of the tree stumps remaining after felling and compare this to the previous photo. Large swathes of Australia's forests have been cleared since white settlement.

Enormous tracts of land were cleared and burned for agriculture during the nineteenth and twentieth centuries, and in the periods 1887 to 1889, 1900 to 1903 and during the later 1920s and early 1930s, records describe koalas suffering from major disease epidemics. These epidemics coincided with periods of drought and could also have been a consequence of severe reduction of the koala's habitat.

White settlers shot koalas for sport and for money, and they became the basis of a thriving fur trade during the late nineteenth and early twentieth centuries. Three million koala pelts are estimated to have reached the international market, although many more koalas whose pelts were damaged or worthless on the market lost their lives.

The distribution of the koala is dependent upon the distribution of suitable habitat. When that habitat is affected by severe fire or drought, koala populations are known to decline. Before large-scale land clearing occurred, koala populations reduced by drought, fire or hunting could have been recolonised subsequently by koalas living in adjacent areas of contiguous habitat. Clearing of great expanses of eucalypt forests has left remaining koala populations to survive in remnant patches of forest. Koala populations surviving in such small, isolated patches are highly vulnerable to the effects of fire, drought or additional habitat removal.

With each reduction in the koala population, something of the species' genetic diversity is lost and a genetically poor koala population is more vulnerable to disease and localised extinction.

Not all koala experts agree on a pre-settlement koala population size, but everyone agrees that the major threat to the long-term survival of koalas in the wild is continuing loss and fragmentation of habitat. Almost all other problems and threats to the koala's survival can be traced back to this.

Present distribution

The national distribution of the koala today is roughly shown on the map of Australia (opposite) which was compiled following a nation-wide survey conducted by the Australian National Parks and Wildlife Service in 1986. It gives a broad indication of where populations can be found today but is not indicative of the fragmentation of many populations within koala regions. The Australian Koala Foundation is currently compiling the Koala Habitat Atlas which will provide a detailed database magnifying current knowledge about distribution, size and viability of populations. Each koala population must be studied separately as each area of habitat supporting koalas differs in size, quality and carrying capacity.

Above: The fertile volcanic soils of this valley made it attractive for agriculture. The landowner has run cattle on this land for many years, and while koalas still survive here, their population has been reduced to small isolated fragments clinging to watercourses and gullies where trees have been retained.

The Australian Koala Foundation estimates the national koala population to be between 45,000 and 80,000 individuals. State by state estimates are as follows: Queensland (25,000 to 50,000); New South Wales (10,000 to 15,000); Victoria and South Australia combined (10,000 to 15,000). Many populations survive as small isolated groups, increasingly vulnerable to fire and habitat destruction. There are no wild koalas in Tasmania, Western Australia or the Northern Territory.

Queensland

In terms of human population increase, Queensland is the fastest growing state in the country; the south-east corner of Queensland, centred around the State's capital, Brisbane, is currently experiencing the highest rate of urban expansion in the country. It follows that Queensland's koalas are most immediately under threat from development. Historically the last of the koala states to be the focus of human settlement, Queensland boasts the largest number of wild koalas, but this is more by good luck than good management.

The largest concentration of wild koalas in Australia occurs in southeast Queensland and northern New South Wales. Koala populations range from Coolangatta on the Gold Coast north to the Atherton

National distribution of the koala today.

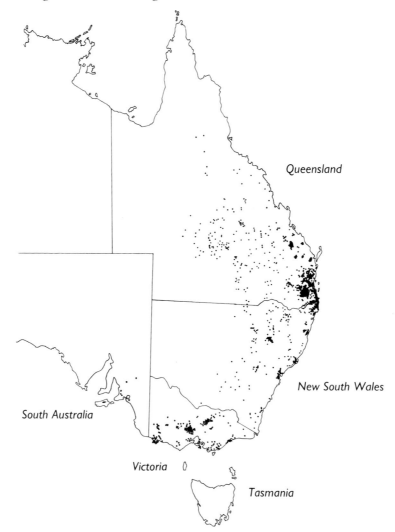

53

Tablelands and sightings have been reported as far west as Cooper Creek on the edge of the channel country in south-west Queensland, but their distribution is not even throughout this range and populations are very localised. In coastal regions populations occur in higher densities than in western areas, where they tend to cluster in suitable habitat along inland river systems and water holes.

New South Wales

Because New South Wales was the first state colonised, its koalas were the first to collide with human settlement. Between 1788 and 1921, 35.3 million hectares were ringbarked and partially cleared in New South Wales, corresponding to forty-four percent of the total land area in the State.

The koala population of New South Wales extends from the Queensland border around Tweed Heads in the north-east, south to Newcastle and Sydney's periphery, although koalas have all but disappeared from the Sydney metropolitan area. South of Sydney, koalas can be found in Campbelltown, and some populations are still found on the State's southern coast, although there is no longer any geographical link with populations in Victoria. As in Queensland, remnant populations occur west of the Great Dividing Range on the western slopes and plains and in habitat fringing water courses. The New England Tablelands once provided extensive habitat for koalas, but with the combined practices of shooting and massive land clearing, remaining populations are small and isolated. The occurrence of koala populations in both the north-east and south-east forests of New South Wales illustrates that koalas do not restrict themselves to open woodlands. Healthy breeding populations

Left: Mother and young, captured on French Island by Department of Conservation and Natural Resources rangers, await transportation to the mainland for translocation.

Right: The relentless spread of new suburbs is arguably the greatest threat to wild koalas in Queensland and New South Wales.

have been found living in old growth forests much coveted by foresters and conservationists alike.

Victoria

Koalas were almost shot out of existence in Victoria during the fur trade years but remnant populations survived in south Gippsland. Clearing of eucalypt forests for agriculture also greatly reduced available koala habitat. Victoria's koalas were given a second chance thanks to the efforts of some concerned citizens who introduced a few individuals to both French and Phillip Islands in Westernport Bay to the south-east of Melbourne, between the 1870s and 1890s.

Between the 1890s and the 1920s, koala numbers on these islands increased dramatically, especially on French Island where the population was, and still is, *chlamydia*-free. *Chlamydia*, a sexually transmitted bacteria, can cause a reproductive tract disease in koalas, as well as urinary, ocular and respiratory problems. Its absence from the koala population on French Island, as well as isolation from human interference, meant that there were no real threats to the population.

In the 1920s, Victorian authorities began a programme of translocation from French and Phillip Islands to other locations within Victoria (and Kangaroo Island in South Australia) aimed at ensuring the survival of koalas in those states. To protect re-established populations, koalas were reintroduced to locations where they would be away from human settlement and threatening processes like fire, so early relocation sites were islands like Quail Island, Kangaroo Island, Sandy Point in Westernport Bay, and later Raymond Island off Bairnsdale. Later translocations re-established koalas on mainland Victoria.

Certain Victorian populations, notably *chlamydia*-free French Island, Quail Island and Sandy Point, have suffered from so-called 'overpopu-

lation' problems, where numbers have exceeded carrying capacity and koalas have begun to eat out the food resource and kill the trees. Individuals from these populations have had no avenue for dispersal into unoccupied habitat since the habitat resource is located on islands.

Observing this phenomenon, Victorian authorities began translocating koalas from these populations and establishing new populations in other locations throughout Victoria. Populations re-established with animals carrying the chlamydial bacteria do not appear to suffer the overcrowding problems of those free of *chlamydia*, since the fecundity of the population is reduced.

Koalas carrying the chlamydial bacteria were translocated onto Raymond Island in the 1950s and despite fears that numbers may have increased to the point where they exceeded the island's carrying capacity, this population appears to have reached a natural balance.

The translocation program could be a contributing factor to overpopulation problems in Victoria, by destabilising the social hierarchy and home ranging behaviour of koalas in breeding populations.

Koalas have been reintroduced into most of their pre-hunting range in Victoria but it should be noted that a wide ranging distribution does

Above: Fertile valleys are cleared for human use while the less hospitable ridges and inaccessible hillsides are left as refuges for wildlife and flora.

not mean that koalas are abundant. Much of Victoria's remaining koala habitat is fragmented and consists of remnant patches of vegetation surrounded by cleared, treeless land.

South Australia

The original South Australian population was shot out in the 1920s during the fur trade. A population was founded on Kangaroo Island by animals relocated from Victoria in 1923. Following this population's successful expansion, progeny were relocated to mainland South Australia where two populations were established in the Adelaide Hills. The total South Australian population is estimated to be 500 individuals.

Captive and semi-wild populations

There are numerous zoos, wildlife parks and sanctuaries that house koalas for public display throughout Australia. There are also some semi-wild populations where koalas have been released into managed parks where they are still essentially captive and receive supplementary eucalyptus feed from the rangers. Koalas have been sent overseas for display and both the United States and Japan currently house perma-

nent captive koala colonies. Additional captive koalas have been loaned to some European and Asian zoos on a temporary basis.

The captive display of koalas raises a number of philosophical questions about the welfare of individual koalas and the conservation of the species. Should animals be in captivity and if so, how does that relate back to their wild cousins? The presence of koalas in numerous captive collections is a reflection of their popularity. People like to see koalas up close and by fostering human appreciation and concern for the species, captive koalas have made a valuable contribution to conservation efforts for wild koalas. But while zoos and sanctuaries provide an educational resource, they are essentially commercial. Breeding programs ensure the continuation of captive stock, not the protection of habitat for wild koalas. Some institutions make contributions to conservation groups but their main priority is their captive collection.

The artificial environment created for koalas in captivity provides food, shelter, health and protection for those few koalas housed there, but is no substitute for the wild. The protection of wild habitats for koalas is the only solution for their long-term conservation.

Above left: In captivity, people can see koalas up close.

Above right: Koalas are much loved by their keepers and the public. They are also a very popular attraction.

Opposite: A contented koala in captivity; his belly full of leaves and barely a worry in the world.

Suitable habitat

The occurrence of koala populations is directly related to the presence of suitable habitat. Suitable habitat has two fundamental criteria. One is the presence of tree species preferred by koalas (principally eucalypts but some non-eucalypts) growing in particular associations on suitable soils with adequate rainfall. The second is the presence of other koalas.

Koalas rely largely upon *Eucalyptus* trees for their food and shelter. They are known to prefer the leaves of certain species of eucalypt, possibly because some are more palatable, nutritious and less toxic than others. Koalas select certain trees for use, be it for food, shelter or social interaction. Two trees of exactly the same species and size can be growing adjacent to one another, and koalas may demonstrate clear preference for one and largely ignore the other. The reason for such specific tree selection appears to relate to factors other than simply the tree's suitability as a source of food or shelter.

It is becoming clear that tree selection has much to do with the social structure of a population and the maintenance of each individual koala's home range within socially stable populations. A greater under-

Above left: Koalas are known to prefer the leaves of only certain species of eucalypt, and they also feed upon some non-eucalypts.

Above: Succulent new leaves — a koala's delight.

BEYOND THE BLACK STUMP By LEAHY & PIPER

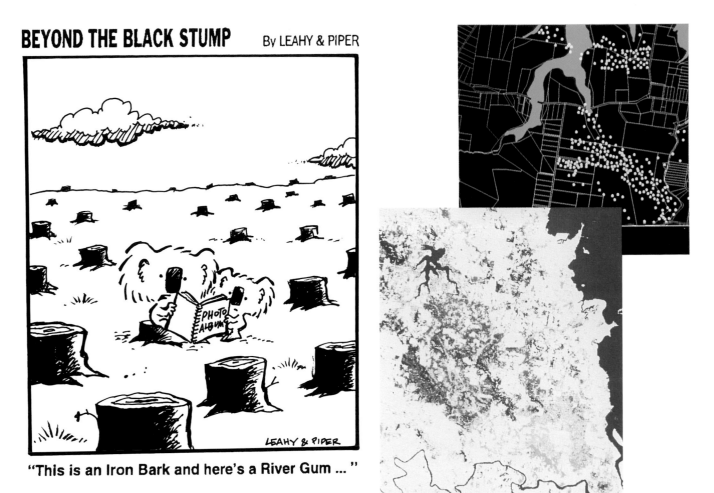

"This is an Iron Bark and here's a River Gum ... "

Above right: Koala habitat is being closely scrutinised and mapped by the Australian Koala Foundation Koala Habitat Atlas. Field sites are selected, information gathered and analysed, and maps showing koala habitat of varying quality are produced. This type of close analysis allows for more accurate planning for the protection of the species.

standing and acceptance of the koala's social behaviour is a crucial factor when identifying suitable koala habitat. Planning for future koala habitat protection and management needs to take such factors into account.

Any given area of koala habitat has a finite carrying capacity. This means that there is a maximum number of koalas that can survive there and any more will simply not fit. If that area is reduced, fragmented or otherwise altered, say by clearing, then there will be a corresponding reduction in the total number of koalas that can survive in that area.

Carrying capacity varies throughout the koala's range and depends on the tree species present, density of tree cover, rainfall, climate, soils and topography. It also depends on the extent of suitable habitat. Trees grow in associations, where particular species tend to grow together under certain conditions. For example, swamp mahogany (*Eucalyptus robusta*) likes moist soils and often grows in association with broad-leaved paperbark (*Melaleuca quinquinervia*), which likes similar conditions. With even the most subtle changes in aspect, elevation, soils or drainage one may find dramatic changes in the vegetation.

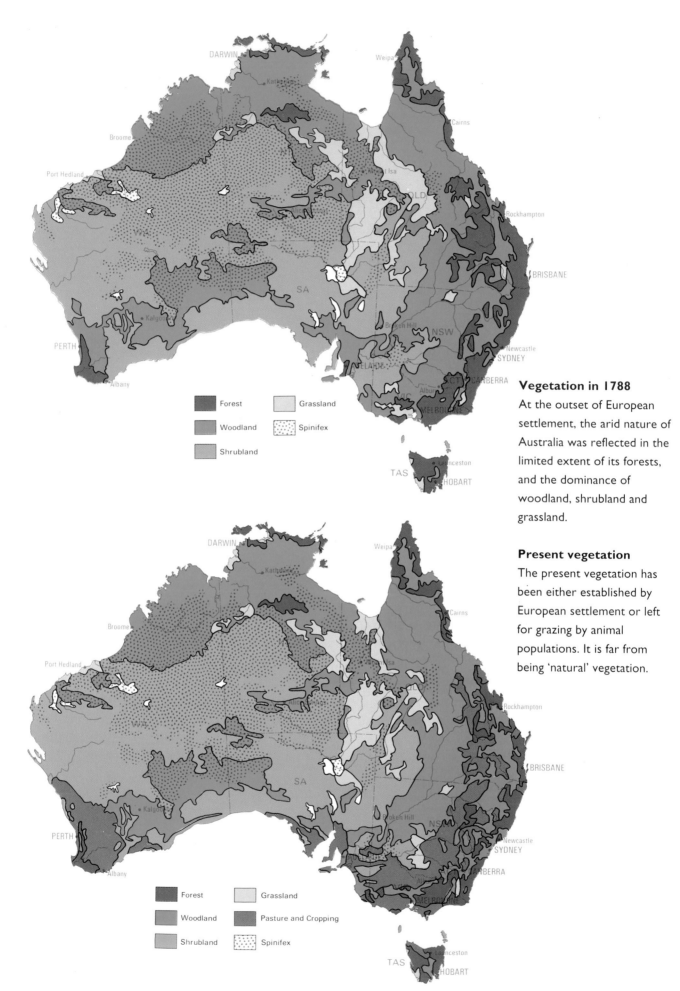

Vegetation in 1788
At the outset of European settlement, the arid nature of Australia was reflected in the limited extent of its forests, and the dominance of woodland, shrubland and grassland.

Present vegetation
The present vegetation has been either established by European settlement or left for grazing by animal populations. It is far from being 'natural' vegetation.

Forest | Grassland
Woodland | Spinifex
Shrubland

Forest | Grassland
Woodland | Pasture and Cropping
Shrubland | Spinifex

62

Above, above right and following pages: A koala's eye view of its environment, the bush.

Close inspection of areas of reputed koala habitat along coastal New South Wales and Queensland is highlighting a serious decline in koala populations. Localised extinctions can result when an area of habitat becomes too small to support a viable population and animals become isolated from one another. There can be other contributing causes for localised extinctions but the disappearance of native fauna from any bushland indicates serious problems within the overall ecology.

Recent field work by the Australian Koala Foundation on its Koala Habitat Atlas is finding that areas once known for their koalas can no longer support viable populations. It is also finding that the distribution of populations is restricted by the distribution of preferred eucalypt species. While this finding is not new in itself, what is pertinent is the fact that one or two species within a region seem to hold the key to the koalas' use of other trees.

Even if a selection of tree species known to be used by koalas occurs within an area, it will not support a koala population, or at least the koala population will not use it, unless one or two critical species are present. These findings are still to be tested throughout the koala's range but promise to revolutionise current understanding of what constitutes koala habitat. They also throw into question the circulation of lists of preferred koala food trees. Omitting the key species from tree plantings to restore koala habitat may be a waste of time and effort.

THE LIFE OF
THE KOALA

Opposite: This young koala cuddles into its mother's belly for warmth, shelter and security.

Above: Young koalas will ride on their mother's back, becoming more adventurous as they grow bigger and stronger.

Koalas have a breeding season which runs roughly from September to March, although there are slight regional variations. In Australia, these are the warmer months of spring and summer and it seems that females produce their young when the trees are sprouting new leaves and there is a relative abundance of food. Captive koalas overseas seem to cycle into the spring and summer months of their adopted country.

Female koalas are polyoestrous, that is they can have more than one cycle during the breeding season, which allows for repeated attempts at conception. It also means that if a female loses a newly conceived offspring, she is able to produce another before the end of the breeding season, but this does not always happen.

If she already has young raised from a previous season, the female koala will not attempt to mate until that young is fully weaned. This will not prevent males from trying to mate her, however, and unfortunate back-young can sometimes find themselves literally in the middle of a fight between their mother and an amorous male.

Left: When mating, the male koala mounts the female from behind, grasping the scruff of the neck between his teeth. A female in season will elevate her rump to facilitate mating.

The average length of the female's cycle is around thirty-five days and it has been suggested she exudes some sort of scent that alerts neighbouring males of her readiness to breed. Koalas produce one offspring at a time, although twins are sometimes born and the presence of two milk teats initially allows the mother to nourish both. As the young koala grows it takes up most of the room available within the pouch and if there are twins, one usually dies. Female koalas have been observed with two young of slightly differing ages which has led to the assumption that some females will adopt.

The breeding season is a time of increased activity within a breeding population and sound levels increase as males bellow more frequently. Not only is breeding taking place, but young sub-adult koalas are forced to disperse from their mothers' home ranges and find their own territory. Where koalas live near suburban settlements, the breeding season heralds the busiest time for koala carers as koalas on the move cross paths with motor vehicles and dogs.

Increased activity during the breeding season and the stress it places upon the koala's body means a higher incidence of sickness. Carers report that more koalas come in for care in a slightly debilitated condition with weeping eyes or 'dirty tail', symptomatic of chlamydial infection. Dominant males fighting to maintain their supremacy and younger males challenging them come into physical contact more often at this time of year and scratches, gashes and bruises are likely to result.

Pregnancy and birth

Once a female koala has conceived, it is a short thirty-five days before the birth of the new baby. When she is about to give birth, the mother sits in such a way, pelvis tilted forward, legs apart and relaxed, that

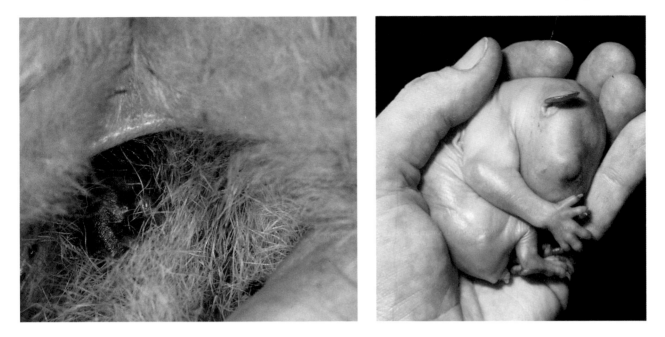

Above: A new-born joey attaches itself to one of its mother's teats (obscured behind the fur). Joeys are distinctly reddish at birth, but this fades to pink within the first 12–24 hours.

Above right: This very young koala was orphaned when its mother was hit by a car. Even at this age, the forelimbs are still more robust than the hind limbs.

assists the baby to make its otherwise unaided journey from cloaca to pouch. The baby crawls slowly towards the pouch, relying on already well-developed senses of touch and smell, strong forelimbs and claws and an innate sense of direction. Once inside the safety of the pouch, it attaches itself to a teat which swells to fill its mouth. This prevents the baby being dislodged from its source of nourishment.

The new-born koala weighs less than 1 gram and resembles a small pink bean at this premature stage of development. It is roughly 2 centimetres long, blind and hairless. It is totally contained within the pouch, which has a safety mechanism in the form of a strong sphincter muscle which the mother contracts to prevent the baby from falling out.

Compared to other marsupials, the young koala's development is slow, due to the mother's strategy of minimising her daily expenditure of energy by spreading lactation over a long period. The young koala relies totally on mother's milk for its first six to seven months. During that time it slowly develops within the pouch; head, body, limbs, toes and claws growing and the first hair appearing. At about twenty-two weeks its eyes open and it begins to peep out of the pouch. It is still a rather skinny, ugly creature, but from about twenty-two to thirty weeks it begins to feed upon a substance called 'pap', which the mother produces in addition to milk, whereupon it fills out and begins to grow in earnest.

'Pap' is a specialised form of faeces which forms an important part of the young koala's diet, allowing it to make the transition from milk to leaves. Unlike normal hard, dry faeces, 'pap' is soft and runny in consistency and thought to originate in the caecum. It allows the mother to pass on the micro-organisms present in her own digestive system which

Left: A seven-month-old joey sleeps peacefully, half enclosed in this mother's pouch.

Above: Around the time of their first emergence from the pouch, young koalas will consume 'pap', special soft faeces, directly from their mother's cloaca.

are crucial to the digestion of eucalyptus leaves. It may also provide the young koala with a rich source of protein.

Koalas have been described as having a backward-opening pouch, in common with wombats, as opposed to an upward-opening pouch like kangaroos. When a female koala first gives birth to young, however, her pouch opening faces neither up nor down. It is a small circular opening centred on her abdomen into which the baby crawls at birth. When the young koala first emerges to feed on 'pap', it leans out of the pouch, stretching it open towards the source of the 'pap' and therefore 'downwards' or 'backwards'.

The baby feeds regularly on this 'pap', and as it grows it emerges totally from the pouch and lies on the mother's belly to feed. Eventually it begins to feed upon fresh leaves, nipping at them as it rides upon the mother's back. It learns to grasp leaves in its hands and before eating them sniffs very carefully. Its early food preferences must be influenced by its mother but its life-long choice of diet will depend upon available habitat when it comes time to disperse and establish a home range.

The young koala continues to take milk from its mother until it is about a year old, but as it can no longer fit inside the pouch, the mother's teat elongates to protrude from the pouch opening. When young koalas are being handraised, the transition from a diet of milk to leaves is a crucial time. Koala carers and handlers substitute the natural mother's 'pap', either by collecting secretions from another female koala producing at the same time, or by crushing fresh faeces and mixing them with a milk formula used to feed the orphaned koala.

As soon as it begins its diet of gumleaves, the young koala grows at a much faster rate, transformed from a thin, straggly looking infant to a filled out, fluffy and cuddly looking young koala. It cuddles into its mother's belly for warmth and shelter but also rides on its mother's back, becoming more adventurous as it grows bigger and stronger.

Young koalas begin to make short forays away from their mothers as part of their development and observations in captivity indicate that 'play' is normal behaviour for healthy juveniles. Young koalas will clamber all over their mothers, regardless of the latter's discomfort, as well as practising their climbing skills around the tree.

Young koalas remain with their mothers until it is time for them to disperse and establish their own home ranges. The trigger for dispersal seems to be the appearance out of the pouch of the following season's young. Mothers will not tolerate their grown young suckling or riding on their backs once they have a new baby in the pouch, but the older young will stay in the vicinity of the mother until the new baby begins to make its first forays away from the mother. If a female koala does not

Below: In captivity, female koalas readily adopt 'back young' other than their own. This mother has temporary custody of another baby (on her back) as well as her own (lower left).

Right: Young koalas learn early to hold on tight, even when they are playing.

Opposite: Mother and young in the wild.

reproduce each year, the young stays with her longer and has a greater chance of survival when it does disperse.

Female koalas are capable of reproducing every year once they reach sexual maturity but the rate of reproduction or 'fecundity' of wild populations varies depending upon availability of habitat, the age of the population and other factors such as disease and decline. Research of koalas living near suburbia has indicated trends towards decreased fecundity and accelerated mortality.

Territorial behaviour influences the breeding process as much as the oestrous cycling of the females. The breeding females of a koala population occupy the best habitat and koalas outside this breeding nucleus are often relegated to secondary or 'sub-optimal' habitat where available food resources are not adequate to support breeding.

Sexual maturity

Both male and female koalas reach sexual maturity at around two years of age but do not usually mate successfully for another year or two. Females generally produce offspring at a younger age than males because older males asserting their dominance force younger ones to the periphery of the breeding population.

It is questionable whether males go in search of females or the other way around and perhaps this varies depending upon the status of each animal within its social hierarchy. Dominant males have to work at maintaining their authority over the other males and overseeing their 'harems', but it has been observed that a female, knowing she is in oestrus, will go in search of the dominant male.

Dominant or 'alpha' male koalas mate with all the females they have access to during the breeding season and will also spend a lot of time defending this 'right'. Other males will also attempt to mate females and even if they succeed, a very interesting biological mechanism comes into play. It has been observed in gorillas (and it would seem that koalas are similar), that due to the superior size of the dominant male's testes, he can flood the female with semen. If he senses that a female has been mated by another male, he will mate her again, effectively flushing out any chance his competitor might have had. This behaviour supports the theory of survival of the fittest; it is biologically preferable to pass on the genes of a stronger, fitter individual to the next generation.

As a point of interest, and further argument that it is closely related to the wombat, a koala's sperm is unusually shaped, with the head curved to resemble a fish hook. This design, while common both to koalas and wombats, differs from other marsupials.

While it is difficult to ascertain the age of a wild koala on sight, its general appearance can suggest an approximate age. This koala, on French Island in Victoria, possesses a singularly 'old' face, that seems to convey wisdom and experience. Some female koalas in the wild have been found to be still reproducing at the relatively 'old' ages of 14 and 15.

Life expectancy

Males generally have a shorter life expectancy than females. They are more often injured during fights, on average they travel longer distances and they more often occupy sub-optimal habitat.

The oldest recorded life-span of a koala was nineteen years, reached by a female at the Lone Pine Koala Sanctuary in Brisbane. Koalas are far more likely to reach old age in captivity than in the wild, however, because their food is provided, they have veterinary care and they do not have to expend energy travelling.

Putting a figure on the life-span of the average koala can be misleading because some survive only for a period of weeks or months while others survive to 'old age'. Koalas living in undisturbed bushland potentially have a greater life expectancy than those living in suburbia, for example. Some estimates for the average life-span for a wild male koala are ten years, but the average survival rate for a dispersing sub-adult

Left: A koala carer becomes surrogate mother for an orphaned koala, which is fed milk formula until old enough to be weaned onto leaves.

Opposite top left: Koalas in care are weighed regularly to monitor their health and progress.

Opposite top right: 'Goolara' — meaning moonlight — is an albino koala born at San Diego Zoo. Albinism, although rare, is known to occur in wild populations.

Opposite bottom: A bushfire lights the night sky. This natural phenomenon has devastating effects on already failing koala populations.

male living near a highway or a housing estate is closer to two or three years.

Natural threats

Today the natural predators of the koala do not make a significant impact on wild populations. They include dingoes, powerful owls, wedge-tailed eagles, goannas and pythons, all of which are most likely to prey upon juvenile koalas.

Drought has been shown to bring on a decline in wild populations as leaves dry out, no longer providing adequate sustenance. Drought conditions are most likely to affect koalas living in sub-optimal habitat away from a regular water supply.

Bushfires have become a serious threat because of the greatly reduced and fragmented habitat areas available to koalas. Small and isolated koala populations are very vulnerable to the effects of fire, which can potentially cause the localised extinction of a population. Koalas cannot escape bushfires; even if they are not killed outright, they suffer burns when descending to the ground to change trees, debilitation and dehydration from reduced food and moisture availability, and difficulties breathing from smoke inhalation. Repeated burning of a region to promote growth of grasses for cattle and sheep, or as a precaution to reduce fire hazards, can severely disturb a population by not allowing it time to recover between burn-offs.

Koalas suffer from a number of diseases and physical complaints
which include uro-genital disease, respiratory disease, digestive tract disease, ulcers, cancers, dehydration and muscle wasting. During the 1980s
there was much public, media and scientific attention focused upon
chlamydia psittaci, a bacterium occurring in koalas which was thought to
cause infertility in females, as well as respiratory problems, urinary tract
infections and ocular infections, and which could ultimately lead to
death.

The focus has swung away from *chlamydia* again and its importance
in the overall conservation of the species has been downplayed. New
scientific work on DNA and *chlamydia* hints that there could be two or
three strains of the bacteria, which occur independently of one another
and which are responsible for the different symptoms.

Koalas are particularly vulnerable to environmental and physical
stress. Koalas have been found apparently starved to death with a stom-
ach full of leaves and the causes of this wasting disease have not yet
been determined. Because they generally store no fat reserves, koalas

quickly begin to break down muscle tissue to convert to energy if their diet is inadequate.

If koalas reach old age, the wearing of their teeth may ultimately lead to their death; if they cannot chew their leaves it is not long before they die of starvation.

Man-made threats

Clearing of koala habitat has already been discussed and poses the major threat to free-living koala populations today. Associated threats include motor vehicle accidents, dog attacks, higher incidence of fire, effects of insecticides, alteration of natural drainage patterns affecting vegetation, and other sundry suburban obstacles like swimming pools and fences.

Koalas regularly crossing busy roads have very little chance of survival, often being hit by motor vehicles. Road kills account for the majority of deaths of the urban koala. Dogs are formidable predators of koalas. An adult koala may be able to ward off an attack by one dog, although it will often suffer fatal internal injuries and die unseen by the dog's owner, but a koala has very little chance of surviving an attack by two dogs or more.

Foxes, an introduced species to Australia, have also been blamed for preying upon young koalas when the mother descends to the ground to change trees.

People tend to apportion blame to motor vehicles and dogs as the main killers of urban koalas, but we humans are the real killers. Our impact on koala populations is immense and in some ways immeasurable. Koalas do not occupy our backyards, we have moved into theirs.

Below right: In urban areas, more koalas are killed by motor vehicles than any other cause. Roads are black holes which dramatically reduce the number of koalas living nearby.

Below: A mother with young on her back. Because of land clearing and human modifications to the environment, koalas are forced to spend more time on the ground, where they are at their most vulnerable.

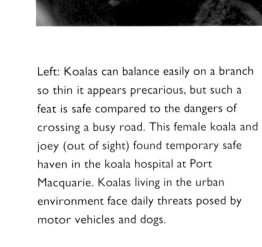

Left: Koalas can balance easily on a branch so thin it appears precarious, but such a feat is safe compared to the dangers of crossing a busy road. This female koala and joey (out of sight) found temporary safe haven in the koala hospital at Port Macquarie. Koalas living in the urban environment face daily threats posed by motor vehicles and dogs.

Above: Such a quizzical face fascinates people and prompts them to learn more about koalas.

SOCIALISATION

Above: A female without young becomes inquisitive at the presence of a mother carrying a baby on her back (in captivity). In the wild, young koalas occupy the home ranges of their mothers prior to dispersal.

Opposite: Koalas in captivity do not have the space to set up home ranges, but when males and females are housed in separate enclosures, koalas will tolerate living in close quarters.

Social behaviour and interaction within a koala population is generally more difficult to quantify than other aspects of koala behaviour. Observations in the field can provide insights into how koalas interact with one another, but more importantly, knowledge and understanding of social organisation can assist the management of wild koala colonies, particularly when they occur in or near urban development.

The signs of social organisation within a koala population are not immediately apparent. Apart from mothers with young, koalas spend the majority of their time alone. Scientific research has now established that koala populations are structured in a complex way. The first settlers, who could see no visible signs of leadership and authority amongst Aboriginal communities, overlooked the subtle fabric which bound Aboriginal people together. Similarly, the initial focus of scientific study on the koala overlooked social organisation because it was not immediately obvious.

Koala populations have a complicated system of communication and organisation which maintains social cohesion. Although they are fairly solitary animals, koalas in stable populations follow a pattern of social hierarchy, establishing overlapping home ranges and behaving in a manner befitting their social position.

MODEL BREEDING POPULATION

Arnie, Marie and Lulu are fanciful names given to koalas M1, F1 and F2 in this socially stable breeding population whose home-ranging behaviour has been intensely studied over a period of 12 months. The beauty of the following stories and hypothetical examples is that the population is real, not made up, and illustrates the social organisation of a small population which is breeding successfully.

HIERARCHY

For the purposes of this story, only Arnie, Marie and Lulu have been named. The other koalas are just shown to be male or female, and numbered M1 (male one), F1 (female one) and so on.

Arnie (named after Arnold Schwarzenegger) thanks to his size, fitness and muscular torso is currently the dominant male in this population. He weighs 10 kg, is probably 4–5 years of age and has by far the largest home range in the group, overlapping with the home ranges of four breeding females. Much of his home range is treeless land, and therefore was not chosen for access to food but rather for access to females.

Marie currently has a weaned baby living within her own home range, and another baby in the pouch. Her home range is overlapped by that of Arnie, as well as another subordinate male (M2) and another female (F3) with weaned young. Arnie's home range also overlaps that of F3 and, like Marie, she is pregnant to Arnie.

It makes evolutionary sense that if you were a female koala, you would try to find the biggest, strongest male to mate with so that your baby carried the strongest genes. Arnie is 10 kg of muscle — a magnificent specimen of a koala; strong, fit and healthy.

Lulu, the female numbered F2, travelled approximately 1 km (a long way for a little koala) out of her own

If the social structure is destabilised in some way, the group suffers. We witness similar chaos within human societies. Wherever the lines of authority are broken down, chaos, violence and disorder reign. In koala populations, where a decline or, conversely, an 'overpopulation' is occurring, a breakdown in the social fabric of the group is often an underpinning factor.

home range to mate with Arnie. We can only assume that she knew she was in oestrus, and, despite the fact that his home range overlaps hers, he was not there when she wanted to mate so she chased him all the way to where he was at the time (in Marie's home range) and they mated there. Unlike males, females tolerate the presence of other strange females in their territory, but not indefinitely.

Look at the diagram (left) and it is clear how the home ranges fit together. You will see males (especially dominant males) have home ranges which are larger than those of females and which overlap with usually more than one female. Arnie's home range is a classic example of the large size of a dominant male's domain; it is 33 hectares in area, while M2's home range is only 17.6 hectares. While much of Arnie's home range is bare of trees, it covers the home ranges of the maximum number of females possible. A home range of this size could probably not be maintained by a smaller animal. During the breeding season, Arnie regularly traverses the length (1 km) and breadth (300–400 metres) of his home range in a night.

This population is a socially secure, stable population, witnessed by the fact that the females are breeding and most have a weaned juvenile in the vicinity and another young in the pouch. This illustrates that the habitat supporting the population is critical to its continued survival. If the available habitat were to be reduced in any way, the potential for survival of each individual would also be reduced. The land is used in such a way as to have each individual animal's home range overlapping with its neighbour. They fit neatly together like a jigsaw puzzle.

The boundaries of the animals F4, M4 and F6 are defined by the creek line, and they abut those of their neighbouring koalas.

Continuing study shows how the animals interact with one another. For example, Arnie and M2 share a tree in common with Marie, which could suggest that their ranges 'overlap' but, in reality, they never visit that tree at the same time. There is no confrontation and they are careful to avoid one another, but the tree is common nevertheless and serves to allow them to maintain large enough home ranges.

Koalas are popularly thought to use mainly eucalyptus trees, but by looking at every tree, regardless of species, field work for the Koala Habitat Atlas is beginning to show that koalas spend just as much time in species of non-eucalypts as they do in eucalypts. They may not eat as much foliage from other trees, but they are using them nonetheless. This illustrates the importance of knowing exactly which trees koalas use so as not to attempt to protect the wrong ones, or protect an inadequate number of trees. Some trees provide a cool resting place on a hot day rather than food, a role which is equally important to the koala's whole life.

The female F5 lives in an area of old growth melaleuca forest and the diet she eats is quite different to Marie's, who lives in an area predominantly of grey gums. F5's young daughter shares the same home range with her. It would seem that young learn their dietary preferences from their mothers, as their first taste of food other than mother's milk comes from the trees they visit while on their mother's back.

A very interesting thing happened during the course of the study which concerned Lulu, F2, the female who chased Arnie to mate. She swam the creek and travelled south, covering a distance of approximately 2 km. She stayed in the vicinity of her destination for a day or two and then returned, covering the 2 km and swimming the creek again to return to her own home range. She made this foray on four different occasions in the space of one month. We do not know the reason for this, but our hypothesis is that she may have been visiting her mother's home range — the place where she grew up — possibly to show Mum the new baby in her pouch. This is only speculation, but it makes a lovely story.

Home ranges

Each animal establishes its own home range, which varies in size depending on a number of factors including habitat quality, sex, age, social status and the carrying capacity of the habitat.

The home range of a koala in a socially stable population is of a size which contains enough trees of the right species to provide adequate

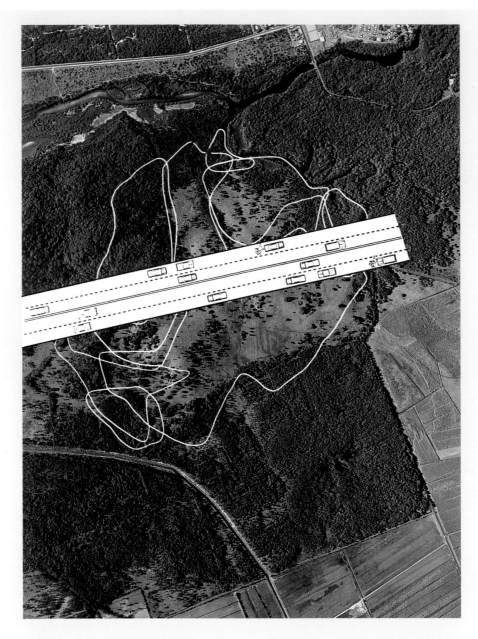

HYPOTHETICAL CASES: FOUR-LANE HIGHWAY

The diagram above illustrates how a four-lane highway would seriously affect this koala population. For the purposes of this example, we have placed it arbitrarily through the middle of the population, but no matter where it is placed, if it cuts through a breeding population such as this, a road will have a major impact.

It is easy to see how such a road would cut off contact between Arnie (M1) and Lulu (F2) as well as Arnie and F4. It would also cut off contact between M2 and F5. It cuts through the home ranges of M2, F5, M3, Arnie (M1), Lulu (F2) and F4 — more than half the population. If they survived the initial impact of building the road, not only would the area available to each of them be reduced, but their normal ranging movements would bring them into direct contact with the road and motor vehicles. For any koala living adjacent to a road, it is only a matter of time before it will be hit by a passing car or truck.

When something like a road is built through their habitat, koalas do not just move away for a while and then return later. Adjoining habitat is already occupied and surviving koalas will stay 'at home', trying to survive on a greatly reduced food resource and in constant danger of being run over. Those koalas not directly affected by the road will be gradually affected by the dissolution of the social group to which they belong.

If koala populations are to be protected, their home ranges must also be protected.

food and shelter for that particular individual. There is an increasing volume of data which suggests that, notwithstanding catastrophe or habitat disturbance, a koala's fidelity to its particular home range may extend throughout its life. Koalas regularly move between their home range trees to feed, to shelter and to maintain social contact with other koalas. This allows for regeneration of leaves which provide the animal's food, and for the regular scenting or marking of home range trees to indicate ownership. Koalas do not remain in a tree until they have exhausted its food supply unless there is something wrong.

In a stable koala population, home range areas typically overlap or adjoin those of other koalas. The home ranges of males tend to overlap those of one or more females, and while they may overlap those of other males, contact will be avoided. The home ranges of female koalas overlap those of both males and females, and young koalas generally occupy the home ranges of their mothers prior to dispersal.

HYPOTHETICAL CASES: CORRIDOR

The 'corridor' marked here was almost a reality. The local council which governs the area where this koala population lives, drew a 'wildlife corridor' on the map which was to be retained to support the koala population on the site. The whole area occupied by the population was to be given over to a housing development. The proposed corridor was 120 metres wide, a seemingly generous donation of space, and from a lay-person's perspective, could be assumed to support koalas.

Such planning decisions are made regularly with little understanding of simple biology. The trees in the proposed 'corridor' were not even the right species to support koalas, let alone cover an adequate acreage to support a population.

Had this 'corridor' of land been retained and the rest of the site cleared, the koala population would have been destroyed. Alone, it is not even the size of Arnie's home range, and it would not have facilitated the movement of the local koala population as it was supposedly designed to do.

Without understanding the koala's home ranging behaviour, it is clear how easily decisions can be made to protect the wrong places.

Left: The burden of motherhood. Young will stay with their mothers from anywhere between 12 months to three years, depending on how soon the mother has her next young.

The trees which mark the borders of a koala's home range are visited regularly and repeatedly by that individual throughout its life. Home range trees can be identified by a heavy pattern of scratchmarks and the presence of good numbers of koala faecal pellets at the base. Such trees are considered to be critical to maintaining social cohesion and appropriate levels of interaction within a population.

Some, but not all of these trees are the places where social interaction takes place. Although it is not always easy to discern which of the home range trees are designated by koalas as places of social interaction, the signs are obvious to them. These trees are critical for the continuation of the population as they are where mating takes place. Without them, koalas would not meet and reproduction would not continue. They could be described as 'bedroom trees'.

Male koalas mark their trees using the scent gland located on their chests. Females have no such scent gland, but perhaps the smell of their urine indicates their territory or home range to other koalas.

Not every koala food tree within the boundaries of a koala's home range is used but they are largely unavailable to other koalas, regardless. This method of self-regulation which koalas have evolved to maintain balance within their populations explains why young animals are forced to disperse from the home ranges of their mothers. If they were to stay, they would compete for the mother's food supply. Similarly if they moved into another animal's territory, they would put pressure on that animal's food supply. The young koala must disperse to an unoccupied area of suitable habitat large enough to provide for its dietary needs and adjoining other koalas' home range areas to maintain social contact with the population.

Breeding females tend to occupy areas of higher quality habitat due to the added energy demands associated with raising offspring, while

dominant males tend to position themselves adjacent. Younger, socially inferior animals arrange themselves around the breeding nucleus of the population.

The home ranges of male koalas tend to be larger than those occupied by females. There are multiple reasons for this. A male koala must eat more to maintain its body size, its territory generally overlaps those of several females for mating purposes, and in areas of sub-optimal habitat a larger area is required to provide adequate nutrition.

When a home range becomes vacant due to the death of its occupant, another animal will move in to replace it, and its boundaries will remain almost the same, defined as they are by its neighbours. Young dispersing males have been observed to hover around the outskirts of a breeding population for a period of months before they establish a permanent home range. These transients will potentially be the ones to take over the home range of a recently deceased male. Males observed fighting in the wild are most likely to be fighting over possession of such a home range.

Below: One koala sleeps on oblivious to the antics going on behind her.

Dispersal

Young koalas remain with their mothers for some time after they are weaned but eventually they must disperse to establish their own home

range. Observations suggest that the timing for dispersal could be the out-of-pouch appearance of the female's next offspring. Researchers have found dispersing juveniles to belong to three principle age classes; roughly eighteen months, two years and three years of age. This observation indicates that reproduction is not an annual event for all females.

Dispersing juveniles seek a suitable area of habitat that is both unoccupied and close to other koalas. As male koalas prefer to select home ranges that overlap those of females, their search is slightly more difficult.

Young koalas seeking their own home range are sometimes forced to cover large distances before they find an unoccupied area of suitable habitat. Dispersal allows for genetic exchange between neighbouring breeding populations and is important for maintaining genetic diversity within populations.

In many areas of koala habitat today, dispersal is hindered by development activity. Available habitat has been reduced and fragmented so that many dispersing juveniles are unable to find suitable vacant habitat. One of two things then happens. Either they die because they disperse into an area which cannot support them, or they are forced to live like vagrants within the boundaries of an established population. This can lead to overbrowsing of the available food supply, the death of trees and a decline in the population.

Most adult koalas spend the majority of their time alone.

Tucki Tucki

Some of the theory associated with home ranging behaviour and socially stable breeding populations came from the study of a relatively small population of free-ranging koalas at a place called Tucki Tucki, near Lismore on New South Wales' north coast.

A group of concerned residents decided to replant koala habitat on an area of old farmland to reintroduce wild koalas into the area. A population was established and monitored by the local residents, wildlife rangers and scientists. Around 1976 observers noticed that the koala population had increased to what was considered to be the maximum capacity for the area. Fearing the animals would continue to breed and create pressure on the trees by overbrowsing as had been witnessed in Victorian island populations, it was decided to relocate some of the animals elsewhere to prevent overpopulation.

From a population of 120 animals, twenty-eight were relocated. Contrary to the expectations of the authorities concerned, the population did not continue to increase but instead began to decline dramatically and continued to do so over successive years.

This was not caused by loss of habitat. In fact the habitat resource increased through further replantings during this time. There was

insignificant incidence of disease, no recorded motor vehicle deaths or attacks by dogs. The authorities were baffled and began introducing new koalas into the population from elsewhere to reverse the decline, but still it continued. The only event that can be attributed to the shrinking population, was the removal of those twenty-eight animals.

The best explanation seems to be that the stability of the social hierarchy within this population was upset by the removal of key animals and without obvious 'leaders' and established residents the other koalas were thrown into confusion and disarray. The removal of animals was undertaken without consideration of their position within the social structure of the population. If dispersing juveniles had been removed rather than mature animals with established home ranges, the population may have remained stable. Studies of Tucki Tucki and other koala populations have confirmed this theory, and could explain the difficulties experienced by Victorian authorities in the management of their island koala populations.

Koala populations can only be maintained where the breeding proportion of the population is socially stable and where there is adequate available habitat for dispersing sub-adults. These lessons must be applied for effective koala management to be achieved.

We must learn from past mistakes
Of all remaining koala habitat in Australia today, approximately eighty percent occurs on privately owned land. This simple fact illustrates that

Above: This vet has a baby koala on her shoulder who is 'yipping' softly. All the mother koalas in the enclosure at that time came down from their perches to check that everything was alright.

if koalas are to be conserved, we must find effective ways to live in harmony with them and their requirements. Urbanisation is currently the greatest threat to the wild koala.

The reasons for the koala's decline in urban populations have been well researched and documented, and planners and government decision-makers have put some mechanisms in place to attempt to protect koalas and koala habitat. Despite this, an alarming decline has continued, resulting in localised extinctions and illustrating the failure of management measures implemented so far. They have failed because they have not made adequate provision for the koalas' home ranging behaviour.

If the building of a road or housing development, or any other clearing of trees, removes the home range trees of an individual, it is rendered homeless. If it is not killed during the removal of the trees, it will be forced to find a new home range. Animals are often observed to return, disoriented, to bare earth where their trees once stood. If half the home range trees of an individual are removed, it will continue to visit its remaining trees but its food resource will have been effectively halved. If it is unable to expand its home range because of intrusion into a neighbouring home range or the absence of available habitat, it will suffer debilitation and possibly death.

'Wildlife corridors' have become a standard attempt by planners to leave some space for wildlife in urban developments. The reasoning behind retention of vegetation for a wildlife corridor is that animals

Below: Koalas live in areas that have become coastal towns and city suburbs: we are moving our backyards further and further into theirs. Today, koalas must negotiate roads, houses and fences, not to mention traffic, to survive.

will use it as a 'green highway' to move from one bush fragment to another. The flaw in this reasoning is that for animals like koalas, individuals in a stable population do not roam in a haphazard fashion but live mainly within the boundaries of their home ranges. A strip of vegetation will rarely incorporate the home range of one animal, let alone a whole population.

Put forward as a 'solution' for wildlife protection in urbanised areas, the placement of corridors is generally dictated by the design of the development (it is usually land that is difficult to build upon or land along the edges of boundaries), rather than the real needs of the wildlife. Another problem with 'corridors' is that often they are the only pieces of bushland retained when land is cleared for development, and therefore lead nowhere.

Roads are 'black holes' for koalas despite some claims that 'tunnels' are a solution for minimising koala road fatalities. Tunnels could not work unless there were a tunnel for each individual koala and fencing along the entire length of road to prevent koalas from crossing above ground. If a tunnel is adjacent to the trees in one koala's home range, no other koala is likely to have access to it.

An understanding of the koala's social and home ranging behaviour leaves no excuse for ineffective protective measures. Knowledge of home ranging behaviour illustrates that if home range or social trees are removed, the fabric of koala society is broken down and it explodes the

Above left: Road widening and logging look more dramatic than well-established suburbia, but they are part of the same process; a process devastating to native wildlife such as koalas.

Opposite and right: Koalas living in suburbia suffer because people do not appreciate their real needs, and are not careful enough about making provision for them when planning new developments.

myth that koalas can just 'move away' when habitat is cleared and return when the trees grow back.

Knowledge of home ranging behaviour illustrates that habitat occupied by breeding populations is crucial to their long-term survival and to remove it can send the population into decline. Koala populations surviving in fragmented habitat pockets amid suburbia are unlikely to be sustainable unless they are continually replenished by the recruitment of animals from a nearby breeding population.

If home range trees are carefully identified and preserved and measures put in place to minimise or erase the possibility of loss by car or dog, koala populations potentially could survive long term in suburban settings, but there are no guarantees. The nature of humans is to do what they please and even with laws and regulations there will always be someone who breaks them. Koalas living in suburbia suffer because people do not appreciate their real needs and are not careful enough about making provision for them.

Future management

The socio-biology of koalas is a critical aspect of the species' management and conservation which is largely overlooked or otherwise ignored in planning studies dealing with environmental impact assessments.

Management strategies should aim at identifying the areas with populations where stable social structures exist. These areas rarely follow the straight lines drawn to delineate the boundaries of land ownership; rather, they reflect the way koalas organise their home ranges to incorporate adequate numbers of trees and interaction with other koalas. They can be identified by the regular and repeated use of trees within a home range area as opposed to nomadic behaviour.

It may be possible to minimise the impact of habitat destruction and fragmentation by identifying and protecting home ranging trees, but the best way to preserve koala populations is not to disturb them at all.

Other behaviour patterns

Zoo keepers and wildlife carers who look after koalas agree that each koala has a different personality and there is no reason to assume this is any different in the wild.

Young koalas 'play' in captivity and carers of orphaned koalas set aside 'playtime' for their energy-filled, inquisitive charges. 'Play' behaviour is easy to observe in captive situations, but not so easy in the wild. Knowing that koalas are most active at night, and not wanting to witness modified behaviour caused by shining lights in their eyes, a group of researchers wore night-vision goggles to observe koala behaviour. They watched mothers playing affectionately with their weaned young and in one case a young male returned to its mother's home range after dispersal, apparently to 'socialise' with his mother.

These koalas rely on the benevolence of humans for their future survival.

In captivity, koalas can display gregarious behaviour because they are more closely confined and live in far higher densities than in the wild. Captive koalas can be viewed essentially as domesticated animals, although they retain certain social behaviours of their wild counterparts. Before much was known about them, people thought that koalas kept in captivity, handraised or kept in home care would be unable to revert to the wild. With experience and examples, this has been shown not to be the case; captive koalas revert readily to a wild state with few exceptions.

Koalas exhibit territorial behaviour in captivity, albeit within close confines. Male koalas housed together will establish a hierarchy. Whenever the tree perches are scrubbed down and disinfected (which must be done in captivity for reasons of hygiene) that hierarchy must be re-established and re-communicated because scent indicators have been removed. Aggressive behaviour and bickering occurs until the markers of hierarchy have been replaced. When this is done, conditions settle down again.

Another readily observable captive behaviour is the bellowing that occurs when the new leaves are being put out by keepers. It is as if they are again reinforcing their own territory, saying, 'these are my leaves because this is my space'.

KOALAS AND PEOPLE

Relations between people and koalas have fluctuated considerably over the years and are largely responsible for the predicament the koala finds itself in today. Prior to European colonisation, the Aboriginal people did not single out the koala as anything more or less important or notable than any other animal in the environment; it was just one small fragment of their whole world. After 1788, however, all that changed. Regarded as a curiosity by early settlers, the koala soon became exploited as a fur resource. Its appearance and demeanour lent inspiration to children's stories, it gained popularity as an important part of Australia's heritage and it has become an internationally recognised symbol of Australia, promoting both tourism and conservation.

Responsibility for the various roles artificially bestowed upon the species rests squarely on human shoulders. We have simultaneously raised the koala up high in our estimation and lowered its chances of survival. In our dreams we are kind to the Australian 'teddy-bear' but in reality we are robbing it of its food and shelter. Fascination for koalas and their unequivocal acceptance of our presence doesn't seem to allay the fact that today people are the koala's greatest enemy. Ours is a love-hate relationship of far-reaching consequence — the koala's survival depends upon our benevolence.

At the time of white settlement, Australia's Aboriginal people had been living with koalas and all other native fauna in much the same way for tens of thousands of years. The new immigrants did not place much value on the native Australians' view of the land, its plants and wildlife. Aboriginal understanding, therefore, was absent from early written accounts of koalas which described a peculiar and exotic animal. The affection with which koalas are described today was also missing. An 1810 account by George Perry, in his book *Arcana*, described the koala as having a "clumsy, awkward appearance and void of elegance in the combination". He also observed that, "... they have little either in the character or appearance to interest the Naturalist or Philosopher."

How opinions have changed! The way koalas have been treated over the years reflects the changes and variations in the way people perceive the natural world.

Aboriginal people hunted koalas both for food and fur but in each instance only for their immediate use. Sustainability was a way of life then, not a public relations exercise. Certain theorists believe that koala

Below left and below: Aboriginal people hunted koalas both for food and fur; they were an easily caught source of protein. Note the size of the koala over the hunter's shoulder (below left) — it's as big as the wallaby.

Right: This artist's impression of a koala, from Perry's *Arcana* (published 1810), depicts an animal devoid of the cuteness bestowed upon it today.

KOALO.

numbers were kept relatively low by Aboriginal hunting practices before white settlement and expansion forced them away from traditional lands. This theory holds that koala numbers increased dramatically when this hunting pressure was removed until colonists realised how easy and profitable it was to hunt koalas for the fur trade. In the absence of a koala census at this time, however, it is difficult to know.

Stories about koalas provide an interesting gauge of how they appear in people's eyes and how perceptions vary. Stories also provide an insight into the storyteller's wider beliefs.

Aboriginal people did not have a written language but their stories and legends are part of a living oral tradition. There are various legends about the koala, and like many animals it is a common totem symbol. Those people whose totem it is are forbidden to kill koalas, but this rule only applies to them.

The following story, told by Bundji, is called 'The Koala's Tail'.

One day
when the world was younger
but not so younger
and the sun shone down
on the sparkling sea
that washed Warrana
Kunduk the Koala
was hanging in his tree
(in that time the koala
had a long bushy tail,
like that one
in South America).

The other birds and
animals
chirped and chattered
about their business
among the bluegums
and the banksia bushes.

The cicadas sang
but the waterdips
in the sandstone cliffs
were low.

Suddenly there came
a rumbling
like Daramalan
with his bull-roarer,
the sky darkened, and
out of it fell a great
bolt of flame
that set the forest alight
after the long hot summer.

High up in his tree,
Kunduk first saw the wall of flame
approaching,
scrambling down to the ground
he dipped his tail into the water hole
and whirled it round and round
like the bullroarer
to put out the flames.

Aboriginal hunters were
skilled at scaling the tall
eucalypts to catch prey such as
koalas, possums and birds.

From a paper given by Fay
Nelson (see bibliography).

But the waterdips were low
and the fire grew and grew.
Quickly the fire spread.

The animals didn't realise
how large this fire would be.
Many perished.

Kunduk's long brushy tail
itself caught fire
and was burnt right off.

Suddenly less encumbered
he turned and ran
losing his tail
driven from his treetops
but surviving.

The fire died down
and Kunduk sat
and thought of what he had endured

and one day went back
— slowly now without his tail —
to the rocky walls of Warrana
saw again the sparkling sea
saw bush and the banksia bushes
grown again
and different birds and animals
going about their business.

They were surprised
to see him there
without his tail
a pale reflection
of his former glory

but when they heard his tale
heard how he had fought
saw how he had survived

they sat and thought
in conference
how there was room in the
bush made new
for them all.

Dreamtime stories such as this are passed on by word of mouth and serve to teach people about the world they live in. The Dreamtime is an all-encompassing term which describes the time of creation and which extends to the present. Many of the characters described are the spirits

103

of landforms as well as living creatures (everything to do with the land is alive in Aboriginal belief) and the stories tell about creation and the natural world.

The reference to drought and bushfire and the bush's capacity for rejuvenation tells of the cyclical nature of life and all living beings' acceptance of that. The Aboriginal world view which held that all beings, the animals, the plants and people, were part of the whole Dreamtime creation, was not recognised by European settlers, who saw Australia and its inhabitants as something foreign and remote to their understanding of the world.

They saw Australia through European eyes; unaccustomed to the landscape and what filled it, and in order to extract meaning from their new experiences, they compared it to Great Britain. Animals new to them were viewed as aberrations of known species and in early accounts the koala was variously likened to the monkey, lemur, bear and sloth.

It is a peculiarly western view that separates and detaches things from their natural surroundings in order to study them in isolation, (this book itself is a good example of such a concept). Koalas were originally

Left: Hunters with koala skins pinned to the wall. Old-timers tell stories of their guns 'running hot' when they were shooting koalas and possums for their fur.

Right: A truck laden with koala pelts for export. Over 3 million koalas were shot in the 1920s for their fur.

viewed by European settlers as one more oddity of the island continent and it was a long time before people began to think of the koala as a part of the Australian bush. It is pertinent to note that political thinking has still not caught up. By 1937 the koala had been made a protected species in all states, but today its habitat (everything that gives it life) is still not protected.

Since 1788 the European viewpoint, detached from the natural world, has taken precedence in Australia, and destruction and exploitation of the environment have been by-products of this way of thinking.

Soon after their arrival in Australia, the new settlers noticed the relative ease with which Aborigines could catch koalas, who did not disappear into a hollow or run away to escape when pursued. Koala fur became a commodity on the world market and they were hunted in their hundreds of thousands.

The story of trade in koala fur is not a pretty one and it continued from soon after colonisation until the 1930s. By 1924 koalas were extinct in South Australia, severely depleted in New South Wales and estimates for Victoria go as low as 500 animals. This left Queensland as the koala's remaining stronghold and the focus of the fur trade moved north. In 1919 the Queensland government announced a six-month open season on koalas (and possums) and in that period alone 1 million koalas were killed.

By this time, many members of the public considered it abhorrent to kill koalas who did no-one any harm. Nevertheless, official government thinking held that preserving the koala as a species was of little importance compared to the financial gains to be made from selling its fur.

With record numbers of koalas killed, people began to fear that the fur trade could cause the extinction of the koala. Even the government conceded that koalas were a finite resource. Following the 1919 season and ensuing public outcry, the Queensland government decided to close the koala hunting season, its reason being to allow koala numbers to increase again to provide for hunting at a later date.

During the following eight years, the season remained closed and the government tightened legislation in an attempt to introduce controls to avoid over-exploitation by trappers. Since legislation was aimed at managing koalas as a fur resource and not for the species' conservation, it was not difficult for trappers to circumvent the law which was also difficult to enforce. Many trappers hunted koalas all year round, stocking up in anticipation of the next open season and there was little attempt made by the government to police the illegal trade.

In 1927 the Queensland government again declared an open season on koalas for the month of August, despite much protest and opposition, on the premise that it would win them rural votes. Fortunately for the koala, this was a colossal misjudgment of public opinion and although the open season proceeded with huge losses of koalas (an estimated 800,000 killed during the brief period of thirty-one days), public outrage was so great that never again did a government announce an open season. It also paved the way for the koala to be made a protected species in all states by the late 1930s.

This public outcry illustrates the subtle change of attitude that had been filtering through into people's beliefs. Where once koalas had been viewed primarily as a source of fur for human profit, something had changed in the way people valued them. Koalas had begun to represent something intangible yet powerful — a sense of Australian identity.

Value is a key word here, as it is the koala's 'value' to people, rather than its intrinsic value, that motivates us either to attack or protect it. There are a lot of double standards in human-koala relations and sometimes they are difficult to distinguish. Essentially this is because the koala itself is not in question, rather its comparative worth to us. Battles such as the one fought over the last koala hunting season are fought between people. The koala, when at the centre of rows like this, is an innocent bystander of the conflict and confrontation that occurs between people of differing points of view and different motivations.

People often do not look past their actions to the consequences they may bring. At the same time as the Australian public was showing its support for saving the koala in the 1920s, it was well on its way to destroying much of the koala's habitat. It is estimated that approximately eighty percent of the koala's former habitat has been cleared since white settlement of Australia. Perhaps people did not make the connection between koalas and where they lived then, but today we have no such excuse.

The first koalas to be housed in captivity for public viewing were at

Opposite top: Koalas are the object of fascination at wildlife sanctuaries today. People love to reach out and touch the beautiful fur and listen horrified to stories about the millions of koalas shot for their pelts.

Opposite bottom left: People now see the koala as something to be cherished, rather than sacrificed for its fur.

Opposite bottom right: Koalas have come to symbolise Australian pride.

Koala Park in Pennant Hills, Sydney during the 1920s. Since then, captive displays have proliferated. Koalas make an exceptionally popular exhibit and people ogle and gaze in wonder at the prettiness of their faces and the funny positions they get themselves into. Sanctuaries and zoos provide an opportunity for people to see koalas up close and this is the way most Australians have come into direct contact with them. Seeing them reclining there in comfort, nestled amongst a ready supply of gumleaves, one could be forgiven for thinking that a koala's life is one of total rest and relaxation. It is true that they spend anywhere between eighteen and twenty-two hours a day asleep but wild koalas do not have such an easy life. Nor do they live in such close confinement and relative abundance.

While displays of koalas in captivity provide an excellent opportunity for education and foster a lasting appreciation for wildlife, people should remember that they are artificial settings, created for human entertainment. If our only experience of koalas is seeing them living happily in wildlife parks, it is easy to think that they are all OK. They are not.

In the 1980s the media jumped on a hot new story; that koalas were in imminent danger of extinction due to a newly identified sexually-transmitted 'disease' called *chlamydia*. A story describing koalas as sexually promiscuous was irresistible to the public and it put a whole new slant on the koala's image. As a public relations exercise, it was extremely successful.

Innuendo aside, the media hype that surrounded this new 'discovery' raised public awareness that koalas really were in trouble and attracted funding for further research. It was soon agreed that habitat loss and not disease was the major threat facing the koala.

Australian settlement had been steadily expanding throughout the century and more and more wild koala populations were feeling the pressure. The public, while being part of the problem, responded to the appeal to help, but mainly by expressing their sympathy; while we all want koalas to survive, we do not want to relinquish our own lifestyle.

People are very good at separating cause and effect: "Koalas are so cute and I love them," goes hand-in-hand with, "We're building a new house so the kids have a healthy place to grow up."; and, "Oh that poor baby koala — it was orphaned when its mother was run over," accompanies, "They really should build a new highway to the beach. The traffic is horrendous."

It is unfair to lay blame at anyone's feet but these examples highlight the contradictions that exist between what people think and what people do. After all, we are all human. Essentially people want to help koalas but feel powerless to make meaningful changes to the way society works.

Some people take it upon themselves to act as the koala's custodians; seeking to protect them in their local areas and being the eyes, ears and voices of the koalas should anything threaten their existence.

The koala has worldwide appeal: Germans, Japanese and Americans, in particular, love them.

Following pages: While koalas in captivity, like this one, can relax, safe from man-made threats, wild koalas are still facing danger from us every day.

The appeal of the koala has gone beyond national pride. Koalas are a star attraction overseas, and foreign visitors to Australia, in particular Japanese, Germans and Americans, cannot get enough of them. Perhaps they see something of themselves reflected in those sleepy eyes.

For one German woman koalas are 'totally special' because her life has been transformed since she began a quest to see a real live one. They have led her on a journey of personal growth as well as discovery, and she has visited Australia six times, thanks to the koala's attraction. An American couple spend their vacations in Australia visiting koala groups around the country, helping to nurse injured koalas and forming lasting relationships with Australian 'koala people'.

On behalf of 10,000 workers in her company, a Japanese woman stood up to speak about how she had co-ordinated a koala 'appeal' to help save koalas burnt in devastating bushfires, because she had felt so moved by the koala she had held during a visit to Australia.

Koalas certainly touch human hearts and their ability to mesmerise has a very special and positive effect on people. In places where koalas come up against the trappings of our modern society, there is always someone who will rescue them, patch them up and devote painstaking, heartbreaking hours, weeks and years to their rehabilitation. The trouble is that sheer numbers of people are crowding koalas out of house and home.

Koala, the animal, has the ability to bring people together; koala 'issues' tend to split people apart. We humans need to separate the koala from the issues that threaten to suffocate it and focus on the animal itself. Koalas have a lot to teach us about acceptance, gentleness and harmony and we have a lot to learn.

BE ALERT
KOALAS ACTIVE

SEPTEMBER
TO
MARCH

Ph. 2020200

HOT SPOTS

Without much argument, you could say that wherever wild koalas come face to face with human settlement they come under threat. Our modern lifestyle, with its roads, reliance on motor vehicles, suburban configuration of house plots cut into neat rectangular shapes and separated by fences, obsessiveness with 'lawns' and neat gardens, fear of leaves in the gutter and falling gumtree branches — essentially the domestication of Australian nature to approximate something European — is foreign to Australian natives and in most cases they are unable to adapt to living amid such an altered landscape.

Most people would like koalas saved, but it is altogether too difficult and complicated to consider the major upheavals to our comfortable existence if we were to make the necessary changes to live truly in harmony with koalas. It is possible but it would require people to sacrifice their standard of living.

Because people fear change, and as yet they have not been forced to make it, development of the bush into towns and cities continues unabated, flattening the finite forests that support koalas. Most people don't wish koalas any harm, but what is out of sight, is out of mind. An optimistic view says the strength of the koala's appeal has the ability to make people change their ways, but this has yet to be demonstrated on a large scale.

Far more effective would be government-imposed law. As more people believe in the need to make changes now, more pressure will be exerted upon governments to impose environmental laws which will assist us to make them. We all understand that resources are finite but have a tendency to avoid thinking about them until they run out.

Despite their popularity, koala populations have been declining throughout their range for many years, particularly between Sydney and Townsville. Conservationists, naturalists and concerned citizens are just beginning to see a frightening conclusion to this decline as populations they have been monitoring for years are severed from the core habitats that support them and aged animals no longer reproduce.

The next fifty years will be critical for the koala's survival, dependent upon the decisions we make about land use in Australia. Koalas live mainly along the eastern coastal strip of Australia where cities and towns continue to grow and eat into valuable koala habitat.

Urbanisation has severe consequences for koalas. Firstly, and most damagingly, their trees are cut down to be replaced by housing, roads and associated development. Populations are reduced and fragmented. Then, from a weakened position, the populations are further reduced by motor vehicles, dogs, disease and isolation.

Some koala populations live in old growth forests which are coming under increasing pressure to be logged for their timber and, more wastefully, for woodchips. Koalas also live west of the Great Dividing Range, where land is used to farm cattle and sheep. A combination of these domestic herds and the introduced feral pigs, goats and rabbits is putting the land under enormous pressure. Cloven hooves pack the soil down so hard that when it rains the water does not soak in but forms gullies which erode precious topsoil. Drought and overstocking mean that all vegetation is eaten and there is very little regeneration of the native shrubs and trees. While koalas in these districts are removed from competition for food resources at ground level, their future food

Right: To a koala, this landscape would be like a bombsite: food and shelter have been destroyed and removed and there is little hope of survival.

resources are threatened because new eucalypt seedlings and saplings are hungrily devoured before they have a chance to grow into mature trees.

Government is slow to respond to conservation issues and the decision makers are so far removed from an urban koala's reality that they have little understanding or appreciation of the dangers it faces. The koala enjoys a higher level of visibility than many species but it is still inadequately protected. Currently, there is no legislation in place at any level of government which adequately protects koala habitat. There is legislation which attempts to place some restrictions on the clearing of habitat that supports koalas, but as yet it has proved largely ineffective. It can either be overruled or side-stepped by governments themselves, land developers, foresters, farmers or private citizens. This is because the system that governs Australian society has not yet taken seriously the need or the urgency to protect the habitat that supports koalas.

Perhaps this is because it has not yet recognised the extent of the threat the koala faces. A more cynical conclusion is that to place strong protective restrictions upon the clearing that jeopardises koala populations would jeopardise economic growth itself and the koala is not yet valued as highly as economic growth by society. The sad reality is that unless such restrictions are put in place very soon, we will forfeit our chance to enjoy koalas in the future.

While this may sound like a broad generalisation, the suffering felt by urban koalas is a daily story of bitter-sweet hope and tragedy. In the parts of Australia considered 'hot spots', where the spread of civilisation encroaches into koala habitat, the victims lie strewn in Progress's path. Animals are killed outright or displaced when trees are cleared.

Populations that functioned as a whole through intricate social boundaries and relationships are torn asunder, split up, pieces removed and the whole fragmented into smaller, dislocated parts.

Once the initial impact of clearing is over, koalas face daily threats in the form of cars and dogs. It is estimated that roughly 4,000 koalas die each year in urban Australia from man-made causes. This rough estimate, based on the records and accounts of the many community-based koala groups around the country, comes complete with an added estimate that for each koala accounted for, another three to four die unseen. That is a large percentage to be removed from a national population of between 45,000–80,000. Of course, new koalas are born to augment the figures each year, but it would seem that the overall population is decreasing.

Wherever new housing estates are being built near koala populations, the locals' lament is the same; "There used to be a lot of koalas around here but we don't seem to see them any more." Some individuals may linger on and live out their lives evading the dangers of suburbia, but when they die there are no young to take their places and the population gradually dissipates until quietly, without a fuss, it is extinguished for good.

'Extinction is forever' the slogans say, and localised extinction is just as serious. While animals can be transplanted from elsewhere to boost a failing population, those new recruits will not be able to remedy the situation unless the causes of the decline have been addressed and removed.

Queensland koalas
Official Status: Common

Koalas living here are sitting on a time bomb as, piece by piece, the habitat that supports them is cut down to be replaced by new housing estates and their associated infrastructure. Concerned citizens and conservationists alike are mostly helpless to stop developments, as the law in Queensland favours development. The only state in Australia to include in its legislature 'injurious affection', Queensland compensates land owners for any potential monetary loss they may suffer if their land is rezoned for habitat protection. Even if the local authority (council) is opposed to a particular development on the grounds that it might harm koalas, its hands are tied by archaic state law which enables the developer to sue councils for potential loss of income.

In late 1994, the koala was gazetted as 'common wildlife' pursuant to the Nature Conservation Act, 1992. The legislative implications of this are that the koala has been effectively excluded from the protection provided by this Act for species listed in higher conservation categories. The Australian Koala Foundation disagrees with this classification and

Opposite top: The landscape after a bushfire. While the xanthorrhoeas regenerate, there is almost nothing in the way of food for the koala.

Opposite bottom:
INEXORABLE FRAGMENTATION
The retention of areas of koala habitat able to sustain viable populations is complicated by the fact that most remaining koala habitats occur on privately owned land. Koalas do not recognise artificial boundaries of land tenure created by people, but their future depends on it.

Legislation governing koalas differs from state to state; laws and by-laws determining land zoning differs within each state from council to council, and within each council's boundaries, land is further cut up by private ownership.

The problem for koalas is that their habitat extends over state, council and individual property boundaries, and decisions affecting its use for other purposes (e.g., housing, logging, roads, etc.) are usually made without taking the whole area of habitat into account. This has resulted in an insidious erosion of koala habitats, until what remains can no longer support populations.

A regional perspective is fundamental to effective habitat conservation.

QUEENSLAND

CITY OF
BRISBANE

SHIRE OF
REDLAND

Koala habitat further
divided by roads and
housing blocks.

CITY OF
LOGAN

COASTLINE

SHIRE BOUNDARIES

CORE KOALA HABITAT

117

advises that the species is in a state of decline comparable to koalas in New South Wales.

New South Wales koalas
Official Status: Rare and vulnerable

Today, so much of the state has been modified by human use that it is hard to imagine the majesty of the forests prior to white settlement. Isolated koala colonies occur patchily along New South Wales' coastline and several are surviving with difficulty. Towns like Port Macquarie, Coffs Harbour and Lismore have become famous for their suburban koalas, but despite mammoth efforts by community groups in each place, koalas are suffering terribly because their habitat resource has been slowly eaten away. Port Macquarie's 'town' koalas, for example, have been sustained by a flow of new animals originating in relatively undisturbed forest to the south of the town. The koala population living within the precincts of Port Macquarie is now in real danger of localised extinction because in 1994 forests to the south suffered a major bushfire. More seriously, an approved ring-road will cut the town's koalas off from the source population.

The politicians and planners who have decided to build the road but wish to alleviate public concern have designed a koala 'tunnel' without any understanding of the koala's ranging behaviour. Koala tunnels will never work. There is no such thing as a koala-friendly road — it is just a people panacea to put minds at rest. Koalas cannot avoid being killed on major roads. They may cross successfully a few times, but inevitably they will be run over.

Above: Innocent bystander or culprit? Dogs are major killers of koalas, although it should be remembered that their presence is fostered by people.

Victorian koalas
No Official Status

The 'overpopulation' problems experienced by some Victorian koala populations are cited by some to create an unbalanced view of the national status of the koala and to dismiss claims by conservationists that koalas are in decline throughout the rest of their range.

While Victorian authorities are conducting what they believe to be the most humane form of koala management, were they to allow the populations suffering 'overpopulation' to stabilise, rather than exacerbating their instability by the regular removal of randomly selected animals, the artificially created overpopulation problem may well disappear.

Other places in Victoria that support koala populations seem to have stable populations. There is not the same rate of urban or agricultural development in that state as in Queensland or New South Wales. However, where Victorian koalas come into close contact with human settlement and fresh clearing, the same stories apply as further north. Despite the official view that koalas don't have a problem in Victoria,

Above: Yet another subdivision; and the landscape is destroyed to provide homes and amenities for still more people.

there are Victorians who will tell you, "We used to have koalas around here but don't see them any more."

South Australian koalas

Official Status: Rare and vulnerable

South Australia's koala population is small and confined to Kangaroo Island and the Adelaide Hills.

Gradual decline

There is a point beyond which koala populations can no longer sustain themselves. This point is not easy to define because the carrying capacity of koala habitat varies depending on factors such as soil type, rainfall, aspect, vegetation and nutritional levels. There is no standard formula that can be applied to assess habitat quality. Each koala population is specific to its locality and each koala's home range is unique. To make a realistic assessment of exactly how much and which habitat must be retained to support a population, every piece needs to be studied closely.

The process of decision-making regarding land use tenure being what it is, any definition of koala habitat which is vague and imprecise is open to misinterpretation. Unless planners are provided with hard data on koala habitat, their planning for koala protection cannot be adequate.

There are dozens of examples of unsuccessful attempts to preserve koala populations along Australia's east coast because the habitat set aside for koalas was piecemeal or not necessarily habitat they use,

and/or because such decisions were made in isolation without an overview of the koala population as a whole.

Avalon on the Barrenjoey Peninsula, north of Sydney, is a classic example of the inexorable, well-documented decline and localised extinction of a koala population that is being repeated over and over again in other places. In the 1940s, scientists warned that the koala population would be locally extinct in about fifty years if the loss of habitat were to continue at the same rate. Today, roughly fifty years later, four animals are thought to remain.

The Australian Koala Foundation issued a grim warning in 1994 that unless there are real protection measures placed on koala habitat the wild population will be critically endangered within three generations, given the current rate of decline caused by habitat loss. The Australian

This shouldn't happen, but it does. Koalas, displaced by the encroachment of human settlement into their territory, can be found bewildered and disoriented in dangerous places. What would have looked like a tree from ground level is a hazard to a koala and, of course, no food will be found here.

Koala Foundation estimates that approximately eighty percent of Australia's wild koalas live on privately owned land. This is where the hottest of the hot spots are located.

Coastal land, especially in northern New South Wales and southern Queensland, is currently a magnet for Australians re-settling along the sun-belt where the climate is comfortable and life appears to be easy. This re-settlement is colliding headlong with remaining koala strongholds.

Koalas are less represented on state-owned land, which includes national parks, state forests and undesignated crown land, than on private land. National parks throughout the country support a very small proportion of koalas. Koalas prefer the best land, which has traditionally been used for agriculture and more recently, urbanisation. Koalas occur in some state forests, and there are both ongoing and looming battles between foresters and conservationists as demand forces the logging of more and more old growth forest which supports a range of precious endangered species.

Where koalas are in the front-line versus development, conflict is bound to ensue because of their high profile and public appeal. It is questionable whether the human race collectively will ever sacrifice its own comfort for another species, even one as popular and endearing as the koala; solutions are within reach but only time will tell if we choose to embrace them.

Some people advocate that the only feasible way to achieve conservation of the koala is to buy up suitable land. This is a fair hypothesis, until one looks closely at the economic realities of such a proposal.

The bulk of koala habitat occurs on privately owned land, and much of that land is situated along the desirable east coast sunshine strip. Billions of dollars would be required to buy it and nowhere near that amount of money is accessible to those with koala conservation as a first priority.

We are only just beginning to appreciate how delicately balanced is the koala's reliance on certain configurations of trees, soil type, aspect and rainfall, and how exactly koala populations arrange themselves within such suitable habitat. Following the bushfires which ravaged much of New South Wales in January 1994, and again in September the same year, close inspection of the specific distribution of wild koala populations (or their remains) highlighted that:

1. Koala populations (in those fire-affected places at least) were far smaller and their location more concentrated than previously thought.

2. Available information on the koala's range and distribution was scarce and too general to pinpoint the location of specific populations.

3. Habitat able to support koala populations was specific in its configuration.

The warning bells sounded by these observations provided an opportunity to look closely at koala habitat. The findings also showed up the fundamental flaw in buying land without knowing whether it can sustain a koala population. Several local authorities in south-east Queensland have made much of their land acquisitions for koala conservation, but even after spending an enormous $6 million it has been pointed out that the land is only able to support approximately thirty-five koalas.

With so few resources available to koala conservation, it is vital that exactly the right places are identified before any effort is wasted on securing the wrong land.

Ideally for wild koalas, all future clearing should be halted, but this is not going to happen. Taking into account the distribution of koala populations and the understanding we have of their survival needs, there must be a way of living together. The solutions have already been spelt out in various koala management plans:

- retain home range trees
- leave enough space for core koala populations to survive undisturbed
- lower night-time speed limits
- restrain dogs
- plant trees in the 'right places'.

But one vital ingredient is always missing — enforcement. Politicians are still afraid of interfering with human rights like driving fast and letting dogs run freely in the bush. With enforcement, these simple rules could make the difference between life and death for the urban koala.

Similarly, the enforcement of the National Parks and Wildlife Service rules governing disturbance, logging and clearing in areas supporting endangered species would provide the protection the law sets out to achieve, but economic interests always seem able to override rules for wildlife and the government rarely allocates adequate resources to enforce its wildlife protection laws.

Opposite: Scorched leaves from a bushfire give this animal little choice but to leave its home range area or suffer dehydration, debilitation and/or death.

Below: Tower Hill, a sanctuary for wildlife in Victoria, has become overpopulated by koalas because there is nowhere for them to disperse.

SYMBOLS OF THE KOALA

Today more than ever, koalas are high-profile animals. They have come to symbolise 'Australia — The Nation' and 'Australians — The People', as well as companies, individuals and interest groups seeking to promote themselves through the koala's image. Finally and most significantly, the koala has become a symbol for the conservation of Australia's unique, precious, beautiful and fragile native flora and fauna.

To many, the koala is more than just an animal. It has become an Australian icon, revered by many, thanks to the image that has gradually built up around it. At first glance, the average observer may think the koala is just another sleepy marsupial, but take a broader look at its iconography, the combinations and permutations of koala symbolism, and you will begin to notice how much its image is manipulated to sell ideas, products, propaganda and a conservation message. For better or worse, the koala is Australia's superstar. It is more than a mascot and due to the popularity of its image it is borrowed by many who want to promote a product, an idea or themselves.

Ask any Japanese or German tourist what they most want to see when they visit Australia and invariably the answer will be KOALAS! "Oh so cute, kawaiii" (Japanese for cute). "They are so calm and so beautiful... so peaceful." The koala far outstrips the kangaroo in popularity and Australian travellers are more likely to sport a clip-on koala on their luggage than any other symbol of Australia.

Aesthetics appear to be the main reason for this phenomenon. The koala appeals to the Australian psyche and one theory holds that its fluffy ears and big black nose are largely responsible. It also appeals to many visitors to Australia, and as a consequence the koala is a major tourist attraction.

Of course, to have reached such heights of popularity, the koala's appeal must be more than merely visual. Other qualities which make it attractive to us include its seemingly vulnerable air, the fact that it doesn't threaten or confront us in any way, its likeness to the teddy bear and that even though it has come to be surrounded by politics, the animal itself transcends them with its infinite charm.

Birth of a national icon

During the early years of the twentieth century, when the Australian sense of identity and national pride was beginning to gel, the koala slowly began to filter into the national psyche. In early settlement years, koalas were seen primarily as a fur resource but gradually they came to be recognised as a symbol of Australia and nationalism. Federation of the Australian states into one nation occurred in 1901 and before long koala characters like Blinky Bill and Bunyip Bluegum were born to delight Australian children and adults alike with their mischievous adventures and wit and to reinforce what it meant to be Australian.

The publication and subsequent popularity of children's books like *The Magic Pudding* in 1918 and *Blinky Bill* in 1939 illustrated a new feeling of Australian identity, separate from Great Britain. The fact that the koala was chosen to represent this identity is significant.

Because the koala is a peaceful, non-aggressive and attractive animal, its choice as the personification of a uniquely Australian character offended no-one. The new koala characters were imbued with human characteristics and people began to identify with them as more than mildly interesting animals. They were given names, emotions and human expressions. They were dressed up to look like little people and a connection was formed between 'us' and 'them' which helped to foster a protective feeling amongst readers and admirers.

They appealed to the way Australians had come to see themselves; slightly irreverent while maintaining a moral code, not straight-laced like their English forebears and full of fun. Specific koala characters like Blinky Bill and Bunyip Bluegum were used to represent individual peo-

Bunyip Bluegum and Uncle Wattleberry are koala characters from the Australian children's classic *The Magic Pudding*, by Norman Lindsay.

ple, their foibles and idiosyncrasies. More general, unnamed and often undressed koala drawings or cartoons came to represent broader, sometimes intangible, concepts such as national pride, motherhood, collective bravery and humility.

Koalas as characters speak to people on their own terms and articulate their values. They are used as role models and succeed because they reveal their vulnerabilities and they don't preach. They also point out human weaknesses and show us how our way of life impinges upon theirs. Used in such a way, koala imagery potentially has considerable persuasive power.

The following passage from *Blinky Bill* is a moving comment on the brutality of the trade in koala fur and far more poignant than any statistics listing the millions of animals trapped and shot.

Poor Mr Koala one day was curled up asleep in his favourite corner, when the terrible thing happened. Bang! He opened his eyes in wonder. What was that? Did the limb of the tree snap where that young cub of his was skylarking? He moved very slowly to take a look and bang! again. This time he felt a stinging pain in his leg. What could it be? And peering over the bough of the tree he saw a man on the ground with something long and black in his arms. He gazed down in wonderment. Whatever was that, and how his little leg hurt. Another bang and his ear began to hurt. Suddenly a great fear seized him, he slowly turned and tried to hide round the tree, peering at the ground as he did so. Bang! again, and now his poor little body was stinging all over. He grunted loudly and slowly climbed up the tree, calling Mrs Koala and Blinky as he went. He managed to reach the topmost branch and now turned to see where his family were. Tears were pouring down his poor little face. He brushed them away with his front paws and cried just like a baby. Fortunately Mrs Koala and Blinky Bill were hiding in the leaves, quite motionless, and the shadows of the tree made them appear as part of it. The man with the gun stood and waited a long time, then walked away, whistling as he went — the only sound to be heard in the bush except the cries of a little bear far up in the tree.

One of the many and varied faces of Dorothy Wall's Blinky Bill (above) and the original patriotic Blinky Bill (below).

All that day and night the little family lay huddled together, not daring to move, or to think of the sweet gum-leaves that hung from the tree inviting them to supper. As the sun rose the birds woke with a great chattering, the earth stirred with the feet of small animals running backwards and forwards; but up in the gum-tree a mother bear and her baby sat staring in surprise at another bear who did not move. They grunted and cried, and even felt him with their soft paws, but he still did not move. All that day and the next night they sat patiently waiting for him to wake, then at last Mrs Bear seemed to understand that her husband was dead. She climbed down the tree, with Blinky following close behind, and went to another tree where they had a good meal of young leaves and tender shoots.

"Why are we eating so much?" Blinky inquired.

"We are going away, dear," Mrs Bear replied. "We must find a tree farther in the bush where those men with guns can't come, and as we may be a long time in finding a suitable home, these leaves will keep us from feeling hungry."

From *Blinky Bill* (1939) by Dorothy Wall

An anti koala-hunting message such as this is delivered far more effectively when the koala is personified and we can relate to his fear and distress. The public outcry that led to the end of the fur trade was fuelled by this sort of imagery.

Since koalas were first illustrated to resemble people, they have been a favourite subject for cartoonists. Norman Lindsay, the artist who created Bunyip Bluegum and *The Magic Pudding,* is probably better known for his erotic nudes. Nevertheless, he identified very strongly with the koala and being cartoonist for *The Bulletin* (Australia's national weekly current affairs magazine), he used his koala characters to make social and political comment. Today, koalas still feature in regular newspaper cartoon strips. From such a hallowed position, the koala as a character can comment on anything and people accept its views as a yardstick. What a platform from which to launch a thousand campaigns!

To get closer to koalas in spirit, authors and artists give them human qualities and stylise their appearance to make them seem more like us. The koala as a symbol is more accessible than the real thing. It can help to define our place in the world (traveller/national identity) and represent our hopes and aspirations (Olympic athletes).

The anthropomorphisation of the koala which began with Blinky Bill and Bunyip Bluegum, and the subsequent popularity of koala characters in their mould, has resulted in a plethora of koala images which dance across our consciousness, selling us any number of messages, ideas, slogans and products. The trade in koala imagery has become big business and all it takes is a picture of those fluffy ears and big black nose on a face that approximates the real thing and one has a potent marketing tool.

Advertising and promotion uses the language of symbols to express its ideas and tout its wares, and over the years koalas have become a readily used image in that language. Today, koalas in many and varied forms sell real estate, visits to Australia, political campaigns, watches,

Right: Kenny Koala, an Australian version of Mickey Mouse, is the mascot of Dreamworld, a tourist attraction modelled after Disneyland on Australia's Gold Coast.

rice, cheese, souvenirs, ice-cream, campervans, backpacks, t-shirts, baby-wear, books, postcards, stamps, chocolates, cough elixir... the list goes on.

Koalas sell the concept of 'Australian-made', nationalism, childhood, family harmony and harmlessness. Companies use their image to convey trustworthiness and corporate goodwill. They are adopted by groups as a symbol to fight off development and conversely they are used by developers and land promoters to sell land 'with koalas in the backyard'. Ironically this last type of promotion usually does koalas themselves very little good.

The isolation of the animal from what sustains it, in the imagery and symbolism that is used to promote it, can foster misconceptions and confusion in the minds of the public. Reading the symbol for a koala has become second nature to Australians but most do not look beyond the image to the promoter's objective. After all, we are all constantly bombarded by advertising imagery and there is no patent on the koala's image. If you are worried about the animal itself, beware the propaganda — it may not be what it seems.

Education

Children around the world learn about koalas and they are an interesting subject indeed. Koalas eat gumleaves. They are marsupials, NOT BEARS! They live perched high up in the gum trees.

The koala is instantly appealing to children because of its similarity to teddy bears, an added bonus in the classroom. A conservation message has been filtering into the curriculum in recent years and children

Left: Because of their friendly, non-threatening image, koalas are often used to teach children about conservation.

130

make drawings that plead not to cut the trees down or lament a poor koala's wet bottom (chlamydial symptom). Since Dorothy Wall prefaced *Blinky Bill* with the words, "to all kind children", those of us with conservation in mind have placed a hefty slice of hope in the minds and thoughts of today's children, tomorrow's adults, who will protect those fuzzy, sleepy images of their childhood.

Hope is vital but children grow up to be adults in a world whose gods are money and progress. It is very difficult to maintain one's childhood ideals when faced with harsh reality. Nevertheless the generation in primary school right now has been raised on a stronger conservation message than ever before and hopefully they will make substantial changes in the future.

Conservation

Education reaches further than childhood and the power of the koala to teach about broader conservation issues and to influence anti-conservation thinkers is considerable.

The koala is an ideal symbol to promote conservation because it is non-threatening, inoffensive and the animals do not destroy agricultural crops. In addition, the koala is very specific to the habitat that can support it, and so is a good indicator species to highlight deterioration of habitat. For these combined reasons, the koala is used as a flagship species to represent others that share its environment. After all, how many would be willing to contribute to saving a threatened snake or a native rat? They are just as important in the scheme of things but they just don't have the same pull.

Below: A roadside billboard designed to remind motorists that koalas cannot survive without trees.

The concept of koala conservation enjoys a relatively large following and it has a headstart on most other species. Like pandas, dolphins and whales, the koala can be categorised as 'charismatic mega-fauna', thanks to the broad appeal of its image. It has the potential to reach even greater global heights of popularity than these species because it does not harm humans in any way and resides literally in our backyards.

Tourism

Another ray of hope for the koala lies in its appeal to foreign visitors. It used to be said that Australia 'rode on the sheep's back', but these days more and more people are recognising that Australia could be riding on the koala's back. Tourism has become one of the island continent's foremost industries and koalas are a prime attraction.

Koalas usually feature prominently in tourism promotion. They are a big drawcard and sometime during their stay most foreign visitors to Australia's shores make their way to a zoo or sanctuary to get close to a koala. If the tourist industry as a whole recognises the koala for the economic value it brings, that same industry could become a powerful ally for conservationists.

Public acceptance of the need for conservation has increased markedly this century. The koala symbolises the soft face of conservation, and this facet of its image fits perfectly with the relatively new concept of eco-tourism. Japanese people are beginning to come and plant 'koala food trees' and local authorities and tour operators are investigating ways to cash in on their naturally-occurring koala 'resources'. On the positive side, the flow-on effects to protect wild koalas could be considerable, but danger lies in the potential for exploitation of this natural 'resource' to make a quick buck without adequate long-term planning to protect it. The koala's image is both a blessing and a threat to the sleepy marsupial who is itself oblivious to the fame surrounding it.

Starting as a children's book character, the koala has progressed to become a marketing tool, a teacher, a role model and an icon. Along the way it has been used to promote products and ideas that have nothing to do with it. The selling of a product is relatively harmless, but sometimes the language of koala symbolism is used to deceive an image-hungry public that koalas will survive when in fact the promoter intends them grave harm. Like the wicked witch or the big bad wolf in fairy tales, propaganda promoters play on our need to be told that everything will be fine if only we trust in them.

Politicians at every level, while wanting to bask in the glow of koala symbolism, have been guilty of using it to mislead the public into believing that they will protect koalas, even if building a road or approving a new subdivision will undoubtedly destroy koala habitat. They play on public ignorance of the koala's social, biological and rang-

Koalas are big business for the souvenir and tourist industries in Australia. Japanese tourists in their millions come to experience the joy of touching a koala, even momentarily, before returning home laden with koala 'mementos'.

ing behaviour and pull at people's heart strings, assuring them that they will take care of the animals.

"If we build a new road (read eight-lane highway) the koalas will just move away and come back when it is finished". This is untrue and impossible. Politicians, the masters of thirty-second grabs and phraseology for four-year-olds, tap into our wish that koalas will be safe and we won't have to give up anything ourselves. We must be careful not to be tricked by anti-koala symbolism.

Koalas are great promoters of 'the cause' and can be exploited by those desperate to have their case heard. If you want a public hearing, using the koala is as good a way as any. Protesters sometimes cite koalas as a high profile species present on a site which is earmarked for development when in fact they are not present at all. With rigorous Environ-

Left: There is nothing as great as the love of a child for his or her soft, cuddly koala.

Opposite: Images like this prompt people to help. Something about the koala's young reminds us of our own, and the need to protect them.

Following pages: Koalas cannot survive in isolation from their environment.

mental Impact Studies and Fauna Impact Studies now required in many cases, such false claims may arouse suspicions about subsequent protests. If one cries wolf too often, the koala's cause will suffer from public apathy.

We have arrived at a point which is by no means final; a moment in history where the benefits of the koala's high profile outweigh the disadvantages. Most people feel kindly towards them and will readily support a 'save the koala' campaign without giving much thought to what it entails. The concept of the cute cuddly koala gives rise to public adoration but also to the false perception of the koala as somehow 'domestic'; it is not.

Combined with a conservation message, koala symbolism is beginning to include the koala's environment. For example, the slogan 'No tree... no me' gets the message across succinctly and strongly that koalas cannot survive isolated from their food and shelter.

Public appreciation and understanding of the koala's needs are improving with its popularity and associated publicity, but there is still a long way to go.

WHAT IS BEING DONE?

In the absence of firm commitment to the koala's conservation by governments and their representatives, non-governmental organisations develop and flourish. The koala attracts a diversity of personalities to its cause and as a natural progression both local and national conservation organisations have been formed. Professional people like vets, biologists and zoologists come to the aid of these groups. Other people attracted to helping the koala find their career paths in zoos, sanctuaries, science, fund-raising, public relations, education, administration or the government conservation agencies. Others give their time freely to fight for koalas or wildlife in general.

Koala conservation attracts all sorts of people for all sorts of reasons, most of which are personal. The koala is a catalyst which triggers people's involvement.

Australian Koala Foundation

The Australian Koala Foundation (AKF) is the principal non-governmental organisation concerned with the conservation of the koala and

its habitat. Its focus is national and it raises funds and public awareness towards its long-term aims. It does not receive government funding. The AKF funds research projects through universities Australia-wide. Its major undertaking, the Koala Habitat Atlas, is a revolutionary project combining rigorous field assessments, computerised GIS (Geographic Information Systems) and satellite imagery to identify, map and rate all koala habitat remaining in Australia, at a high resolution of 40 x 40 metres.

Above left: Australian Koala Foundation scientists discussing potential field sites.

Above: Volunteers searching for faecal pellets to check for the presence of koalas.

The Atlas is being assembled piece by piece, on a shire by shire basis, starting with those areas most immediately under threat and gradually piecing them together like a jigsaw of koala habitat. It defines what koala habitat consists of, where it occurs, its local distribution, relative importance and level of use by koalas. The AKF views the Koala Habitat Atlas as the most powerful and useful tool currently available to achieve long-term habitat protection. As each section of the Atlas is completed, the AKF will focus attention on promoting the conservation of identified koala habitat areas.

As an organisation with a national overview, the AKF advises government at all levels on how best to achieve koala conservation. It advocates the strengthening of legislation to protect koala habitat and it promotes awareness and education about koalas to all those individuals and groups it identifies as having some influence over the koala, including schools and other institutions, land-holders, the media, the business world, governments, scientists, koala groups, sanctuaries and the general public.

Because of its high profile, the AKF is called upon by concerned citizens to 'save' koalas wherever they are under threat. This is a huge task and one that needs to be shared among all groups and individuals concerned with the koala. The AKF has chosen to focus on the conservation of the species. It does not rehabilitate sick and injured koalas. That is the realm of the local carer groups. The AKF works primarily to solve the causes of the koala's problems and minimise the effects.

Carer groups

Koala welfare and community groups are local in focus and usually occur in places where koala habitat is impacted upon by human endeavour. They can be divided roughly into four categories:

1. Carers of sick, injured and orphaned wildlife.

2. Protesters and agitators against local development, who foster community-based education and tree planting programmes.

3. Activists who focus upon regionally or nationally significant koala issues.

4. NIMBY (Not In My Back Yard) protesters who promote the koala as a focus to oppose development that will affect their own lifestyle.

Whichever category or categories koala groups belong to, they always begin with the best of intentions but are often side-tracked by internal politics, personalities and exhaustion. Such groups do important work. They are the whistle-blowers, the eyes, ears and voices of local koala populations and they foster an admirable sense of local 'ownership' or custodianship amongst people whose backyards are shared with koalas. This can only be positive.

The media tends to romanticise the carers because what they do is so visually appealing. It's easier to focus on the cute cuddlies than on the

Computer companies and GIS experts play a part in efforts to conserve koalas.

ghastly, gory roadkill victim or the trees that have been cut down. The image of koala carers conveys a sense of hope that people can actually do something tangible to remedy the situation.

Koala carers are a rare breed of dedicated individuals who devote a large part of their lives to the rehabilitation of sick, injured and orphaned koalas. To do so they must be registered and approved by their state government's conservation department. Koalas require highly specialised treatment and round-the-clock care but the rewards of successful rehabilitation provide the strength and encouragement to continue.

Rehabilitation of injured wildlife, in particular koalas, is an extremely emotive area and it is easy to lose sight of, or simply to be overwhelmed by, the magnitude of the problem. There is also a certain danger in focusing more on the care of sick and injured animals than the conservation of their habitat, but it's an easy trap to fall into.

Some groups choose to focus on the retention of koala habitat occurring in their local area, and this work is surely the most important. Sadly, it is the least visible of conservation actions. The concept of 'progress' is so widely accepted in the community, that the relentless reduction of natural resources to be replaced by human-modified environments is seen as regrettable but inevitable.

Community groups also focus on tree planting, lobbying their local authority, and public awareness campaigns. Some express their concern for koalas by direct actions and protesting. For example, in areas of state forest where logging will harm koalas, some activists risk their lives to protest against it. Ironically, these heroic deeds are scorned by mainstream society despite the fact that 'greenies' are trying to protect everyone's natural heritage. The official custodians of our natural heritage (the government conservation departments) often fail to halt its destruction. Someone has to take responsibility. Protesting and temporarily stopping logging is the first step. Long-term preservation is not guaranteed, however, until it has become law.

Government agencies

The state National Parks and Wildlife Services work to protect native plants and animals but this is mainly within gazetted national parks and other conservation areas. Their powers to intervene on private land are limited and their role in such areas usually advisory.

Each state's conservation agency undertakes scientific research programmes and prepares species conservation and management plans. While resources are limited, these agencies provide a wealth of knowledge and information about surviving species.

There are many dedicated individuals who work for the various parks services who have a particular interest in koalas and who contribute

Opposite top: Radio telen.. allows scientists to track the locations and movements of koalas in the wild.

Below: Koalas are caught and fitted with radio collars which emit a signal that is picked up by the tracking device.

Opposite bottom: Wildlife carers, including vets and sanctuary staff, rehabilitate sick, injured and orphaned koalas so that they can be returned to the wild.

substantially to available knowledge and to the care given to sick, injured and orphaned koalas. Being official custodians, they are also responsible for answering public calls when koalas are run over, attacked by dogs or otherwise threatened or harmed. They licence the carers and are responsible for any proposals to relocate native wildlife from one location to another.

While the members of parks services do their best, their effectiveness is often frustrated by inadequate resources and insufficient legislative powers. They generally come under junior ministries and their funding tends to be disproportionately lower than other departments, such as primary industries, mining, transport, social security and so on.

Many koalas in captivity have an easy life in comparison to their wild cousins, and they provide an opportunity for people to see koalas up close and learn about conservation.

Zoos, wildlife parks, sanctuaries

The keepers and veterinarians who look after koalas in captivity are another category of people with a close affinity and love for the animals to whom they essentially devote their lives. They often act as foster mothers to orphaned koalas, either from captivity or the wild, and share many of the same hopes and aspirations as members of the other koala groups. Many make valuable contributions to the conservation of wild animals.

Scientists

Scientists provide answers to questions about what koalas require to survive and how best to help them. A considerable amount of research into koala biology has been conducted at universities and government agencies and much of the knowledge gained is invaluable for conservation efforts. The more we understand about the koala and its environment, the better able we will be to implement protective measures to save it.

Scientists are trained to have a pragmatic view of life, but many biologists suffer anguish as they watch the destruction of ecosystems they have studied. Scientific data collection and analysis are objective processes removed from emotion but many scientists involved with koalas (and indeed other wildlife) form a strong bond with the animal that moves them to do all they can to fight for its protection.

On the one hand, the academic world discourages its members from promotion by simplifying the message for the general public, but on the other hand scientists with a good knowledge of koala biology are needed by the conservation movement to speak up and add weight to arguments for the koala's protection which can be heard and understood by members of mainstream society. Such dichotomy places some scientists in an awkward position, but if they yearn for koala conservation, their message must be heard. Scientists can play a vital role in ensuring koala conservation measures are given a fair hearing and implemented by the decision-makers of society.

Education

All the koala people described above promote education about koalas and their conservation in one way or another. Public awareness about koalas has been augmented considerably over the past ten to twenty years with the raised profile of one koala group after another. The media contribute to this, as does celebrity support.

Studies have found that children's attitudes and opinions are well formed by the age of thirteen, so primary school is the most productive environment to teach children about conservation. School teachers and parents contribute largely to the attitudes and beliefs of the next genera-

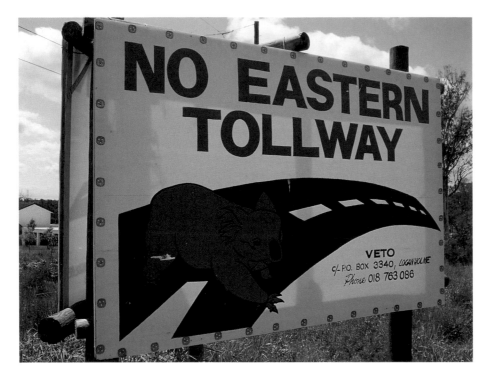

Left: Because of their high profile and popularity, koalas are regularly used as a flagship species to fight conservation campaigns.

Opposite: Many people devote their lives to the protection of this beautiful animal.

tion and many children in Australian schools are learning that koalas need their help.

Others

There are other people, not immediately obvious, who play a role in efforts to conserve the koala. Companies donate money to conservation groups. Shopkeepers sell koala merchandise to contribute to the cause. Television producers, journalists, disc-jockeys, newspaper and magazine editors give koala stories public hearing. Entertainers organise charity days. School teachers, Brownie and Scout leaders and parents teach children about conservation and organise tree plantings and community awareness days. Business people give their time freely on boards and advisory committees for koala groups. Many vets treat native animals free of charge. Shopping centres, supermarket proprietors and shoppers support 'koala-friendly' products. Business people donate prizes for fund-raising efforts. There are many concerned individuals who try to do their little bit for the koalas and the generosity is astounding.

Despite all this effort, the continuing decline of koala populations is telling us it is not enough. A lot is being done by very few and the number of people who don't give conservation a thought outnumber those who do. Sadly, there are even those who work hard to discredit koala groups, creating confusion in the public mind. This is difficult to fight.

There is a lot of good work being done at a grassroots level all around the country, mostly initiated by concerned individuals and community groups. Tree planting, education and awareness programs,

caring for sick and injured animals, fund-raising and attempts to hold back the tide of development are activities which koala groups take upon themselves voluntarily. These activities are very important and valuable, but compared to the resources spent on activities that remove and destroy koala habitat they are miniscule. There is far more promotion given to replanting than there is to retention of habitat. This is absurd.

Conservation is regarded by society as a luxury, not a necessity. It is not seen as something that brings value to society because it is not quantified in monetary terms. There are very few places where highly qualified 'conservation' professionals can make a living and most available employment positions exist within government departments. This means that people most qualified to stand up for the koala's rights and point out discrepancies in legislation are often prevented from doing so because of the firm restrictions placed upon them by the bureaucracy within which they work. To be able to speak freely, one cannot afford to be beholden to government.

Non-government organisations provide a forum for such individuals

Above left: Co-operative efforts, such as one by San Diego Zoo to give aid to the Australian Koala Foundation's Koala Habitat Atlas, not only provide the necessary manpower for field work, but allow for the vital exchange of ideas and learning experiences between overseas and Australian promoters of koala conservation.

Above: Tree propagation for community-based tree planting programmes is wonderful work. Sadly more trees are being cut down than are being planted.

to speak freely but their resources are proportionately small. Conservation groups do not have resources comparable to the economic forces they oppose so they are at a disadvantage. What they do posses, however, is commitment, dedication and determination. Koala conservation advocates could be likened to David fighting Goliath.

In addition to grassroots conservation, the ongoing collection of data and information to support arguments for koala conservation progresses more quietly behind the scenes. It is possible to change legislation gradually with irrefutable proof, by presenting a koala conservation argument in terms the bureaucracy understands. This requires much time and effort, as well as persistence on the part of conservationists fighting for changes.

Compromises must be found between 'progress' and the protection of wild places. Advocates for economic growth criticise the conservation movement for being selfish and greedy and wanting too much, but a simple look at the history of decline of so many of our species of fauna and flora illustrates that 'progress' has been the selfish party.

Despite the dedication of many people over many years and the increasing number of those drawn to the conservation movement, koala numbers are dwindling. We know the reasons, we can offer solutions but there is a certain stalemate and mistrust between conservationists and advocates for progress which is difficult to dispel. The koala's high profile offers to bridge the gap but there is still difficulty finding common ground.

As more land is developed and less bushland capable of supporting wildlife remains, its value for wildlife conservation increases. Owners of

Right: Groups such as the Brownies, Girl Guides and Scouts make significant contributions to conservation work throughout Australia.

Australia's native flora contributes to the distinctive sights and smells of the Australian bushlands where koalas reside. Clockwise from top left: Delicate eucalypt blossom; a proud *Banksia* flower; *Callistemon* blooms light up the bush; bush pot-pourri — gumnuts and gumleaves on the forest floor; a gnarled and knotted old beauty.

Opposite: Mother and baby give us trust — will we serve them well?

such land will find themselves under increasing pressure from the conservation movement to relinquish their democratic rights to profit from that land at the expense of its natural resources. This will foster even more distrust between the pro- and anti-development sides but for the wildlife's sake a compromise needs to be found.

While all development is not going to be stopped by the presence of koalas, it can be modified, and possible solutions have already been discussed. However, an effective management plan for a koala population sharing its habitat with humans has yet to be demonstrated.

If scientists who are truly committed to preserving wildlife long term agree to assess a site proposed for development, they are morally bound to predict every potential effect the development and its future inhabitants will have upon the wildlife. Even if recommendations for every protective measure are followed by the developer of a residential area, it is almost impossible to police the daily actions of the people who will eventually come to live there. Even if protective measures for koalas include speed restrictions on traffic passing through known koala home ranges, there is still a distinct possibility of an accident resulting in the death of a koala. Even if people who move into such an area agree not to own a dog, there is a distinct possibility that one day a dog-owning friend will visit and the dog will kill a koala.

Refusing to become involved in the assessment of a development is equally fraught for the committed conservation biologist because the alternative can be worse. If an environmental impact study assessment is conducted without the thoroughness and commitment of the *true* conservation biologist, potential impacts on all wildlife can be glossed over and neglected, so that the resulting development will not make adequate provision and wildlife will be destroyed anyway.

The dilemma remains. The greatest hope for koala conservation is the strengthening of legislation to protect the koala's trees and supporting environment. This is achievable as long as the truth is told and decision makers listen.

There is still time to protect the koala's habitat using the best available information, combined with passion for the animal itself.

Right: The artist Norman Lindsay loved the Australian bush, and its koalas. It would be a tragedy to lose such cherished fellow creatures.

Following pages: Another day ends with the sun setting over the Australian bush. There is still time to protect what is left of the koala's habitat.

Bibliography

ARCHER, M. *Riversleigh*. Chatswood, New South Wales, Reed Books, 1990.

ARCHER, M. 'Koalas (Phascolarctids) and their Significance in Marsupial Evolution', In Bergin, T.J. ed. *The Koala, Proceedings of the Taronga Symposium on Koala Biology, Management and Medicine*. Sydney, The Zoological Parks Board of New South Wales, 1978, pp. 20-28.

ARCHER, M. and HAND, S. 'Evolutionary Considerations', In Cronin, L. ed. *Koala, Australia's Endearing Marsupial*. Frenchs Forest, New South Wales, Reed Books, 1987, pp. 79-106.

ARCHER, M.; HAND, S. and GODTHELP, H. *Uncovering Australia's Dreamtime*. Sydney, Surrey Beatty & Sons, 1986.

BERGIN, T.J. ed. *The Koala, Proceedings of the Taronga Symposium on Koala Biology, Management and Medicine*. Sydney, Zoological Parks Board of New South Wales, 1978, pp. 20-28.

BLANSHARD, W.H. 'Growth and Development of the Koala From Birth to Weaning', In Lee, A.K.; Handasyde, K.A. and Sanson, G.D. eds. *Biology of the Koala*. New South Wales, Surrey Beatty & Sons, 1991, pp. 193-202.

BLOOMFIELD, L. ed. *The World of Norman Lindsay*. Melbourne, The Macmillan Company of Australia, 1979.

BROWN, R.A. ed. *Planning for Wildlife (Koala) Habitat Protection: Proceedings Workshop 89*. Brisbane, The University of Queensland and the Australian Koala Foundation, 1989.

CANFIELD, P. 'Disease Affecting Captive and Free Living Koalas and their Implications for Management', In Lunney, D.; Urquhart, C.A. and Reed, P. eds. *Proceedings of the Koala Summit on Managing Koalas in New South Wales*. Sydney, New South Wales National Parks and Wildlife Service, 1988.

CORK, S. *Assessment and Prediction of the Nutritional Quality of Eucalypt Foliage for Koalas*. Canberra, CSIRO Division of Wildlife and Ecology, 1992.

CORK, S. 'Form and Function of the Koala', In Cronin, L. ed. *Koala, Australia's Endearing Marsupial*. Frenchs Forest, New South Wales, Reed Books, 1987.

CORK, S.J. and SANSON, G.D. 'Digestion and Nutrition in the Koala: A Review', In Lee, A.K.; Handasyde, K.A. and Sanson, G.D. eds. *Biology of the Koala*. New South Wales, Surrey Beatty & Sons, 1991, pp. 129-144.

CRONIN, L. ed. *Koala, Australia's Endearing Marsupial*. Frenchs Forest, New South Wales, Reed Books, 1987.

ELLIS, J.A. *Australia's Aboriginal Heritage*. North Blackburn, Victoria, Collins Dove, 1994.

ELLIS, W.A.H.; WHITE, N.A.; KUNST, N.D. and CARRICK, F.N. 'Responses of Koalas, *Phascolarctos cinereus*, to Re-introduction to the Wild after Rehabilitation', In *Australian Wildlife Research* Vol. 17 (4), pp. 421-426.

EVERY, K.R. 'Evaluation of a Koala Decline in Population of the Koala, *Phascolarctos cinereus* (Goldfuss) in Ventnor Reserve, Phillip Island, Victoria, by Means of a Triple-Count Technique', In *Australian Wildlife Research*, Vol 13 (4), pp 517-525.

FOWLER, G. 'Black August' — Queensland's Open Season on Koalas in 1927. Canberra, Honours Thesis, Australian National University, 1993.

GALL, B.C. 'Aspects of the Ecology of the Koala, Phascolarctos cinereus, in the Tucki Tucki Nature Reserve, New South Wales', In Australian Wildlife Research Vol. 7, pp. 167-176.

GORDON, G. 'Conservation of Koala Habitat', In Brown, R.A. ed. Planning for Wildlife (Koala) Habitat Protection: Proceedings Workshop 89. Brisbane, The University of Queensland and the Australian Koala Foundation, 1989, pp. 16-26.

GORDON, G. and McGREEVY, D.G. 'The Status of the Koala in Queensland', In Bergin, T.J. The Koala, Proceedings of the Taronga Symposium on Koala Biology, Management and Medicine. Sydney, The Zoological Parks Board of New South Wales, 1978, pp. 125-181.

GORDON, G.; McGREEVY, D.G. and LAWRIE, B.C. 'Koala Populations in Queensland: Major Limiting Factors', In Lee, A.K.; Handasyde, K.A. & Sanson, G.D. eds. Biology of the Koala. New South Wales, Surrey Beatty & Sons, 1991, pp. 85-95.

GRZIMCK. B. 'The Koala', In Grzimck's Animal Life Encyclopedia, Vol. 10. New York, Van Nostrand, 1972, pp. 121-128.

GUNN, D. Links with the Past: A history of early days in Australia. Brisbane, John Mills, 1937.

LEE, A.K. and MARTIN, R.W. The Koala: A Natural History. Kensington (New South Wales), New South Wales University, 1988.

LEE, A.K. and CARRICK, F.N. 'Phascolarctidae', In Walton, D.W. and Richardson, B.J. Fauna of Australia. Vol. 1B Mammalia. Canberra. Australian Government Publishing Service, 1989, pp. 740-754.

LEE, A.K.; HANDASYDE, K.A. and SANSON, G.D. eds. Biology of the Koala. New South Wales, Surrey Beatty & Sons, 1991.

LINDSAY, N. The Magic Pudding: The Adventures of Bunyip Bluegum. Sydney, Angus & Robertson Publishers, 1918.

LUNNEY, D.; URQUHART, C.A. and REED, P. eds. Proceedings of the Koala Summit on Managing Koalas in New South Wales. Sydney, New South Wales National Parks and Wildlife Service, 1988.

McARTHUR, K.'Where has all the country gone.' Caloundra Lunch Hour Theatre Script, 1992.

MARTIN, R. Draft Management Plan for the Conservation of the Koala (Phascolarctos cinereus) in Victoria. Heidelberg, Victoria, Arthur Rylah Institute for Environmental Research, 1989.

MARTIN, R.W. 'Koala', In Strahan, R. ed. The Australian Museum Complete Book of Australian Mammals. Sydney, Angus and Robertson, 1983, pp. 113-114.

MARTIN, R.W. 'Overbrowsing and Decline of a Population of the Koala, Phascolarctos cinereus, in Victoria. I. Food Preference and Food Tree Defoliation', In Australian Wildlife Research. Vol 12. (3), pp. 355-365.

MARTIN, R.W. 'Age-Specific Fertility in Three Populations of the Koala, Phascolarctos cinereus (Goldfuss), in Victoria', In Australian Wildlife Research Vol 8 (2), pp. 275-283.

MELZER, A. and LAMB, D. 'Low Density Populations of the Koala (Phascolarctos cinereus) in Central Queensland', In Proceedings of the Royal Society of Queensland, Vol. 104, pp. 89-93.

MELZER, A. and LAMB, D. 'Koalas and the Utilisation of Woodlands at Springsure in Central Queensland: A summary of research undertaken from September 1989 to December 1991'. Report to the Australian Koala Foundation, University of Queensland, 1994.

MITCHELL, P. 'Koalas on Raymond Island: Distribution and Habitat Use'. Bairnsdale, Report to the Australian Koala Foundation, 1992.

MITCHELL, P.J.; BILNEY, R. and MARTIN, R.W. 'Population Structure and Reproductive Status of Koalas on Raymond Island, Victoria', In Australian Wildlife Research Vol. 15, pp. 511-14.

MITCHELL, P.J., McORIST, S. and BILNEY, R. 'Epidemiology of Mycobacterium ulcerans Infection in Koalas (Phascolarctos cinereus) on Raymond Island, Southeastern Australia', In Journal of Wildlife Diseases Vol 23 (3), pp. 386-390.

NELSON, F. 'The Koala's Tail'. Proceedings of the Conference on the Status of the Koala in 1993. Brisbane, Australian Koala Foundation, 1993, pp.37-38.

PAHL, L. WYLIE, F.R. and FISHER, R. 'Koala Population Decline Associated with Loss of Habitat and Suggested Remedial Strategies', In Lunney, D.; Urquhart, C.A. and Reed, P. eds. Proceedings of the Koala Summit on Managing Koalas in New South Wales. Sydney, New South Wales National Parks and Wildlife Service, 1978, pp. 39-47.

PERRY, G. Arcana. James Stratford, London, 1810.

PHILLIPS, S. 'The Koala and Mankind', In Cronin. L. ed. Koala, Australia's Endearing Marsupial. Frenchs Forest, New South Wales, Reed Books, 1987, pp. 111-127.

PHILLIPS, S. Koala Management Plan for Proposed Searanch Residential Development. Brisbane, report to Ray Development Corporation Pty Ltd, 1994.

PHILLIPS, B. Koalas: The little Australians we'd all hate to lose. Canberra, Australian Government Publishing, 1990.

PIETERS, C.W. and WOODALL, P.F. 'An Investigation into the Factors that Influence Habitat Usage by a Koala (Phascolarctos cinereus) Population in South-east Queensland'. Final Report to the Australian Koala Foundation, University of Queensland, 1993.

PONTING, C. A Green History of the World. London, Penguin Books, 1991.

REED, P.C. and LUNNEY, D. 'Habitat Loss: the key problem for the long term survival of koalas in New South Wales', In Lunney, D.; Urquhart, C.A. and Reed, P. eds. Proceedings of the Koala Summit on Managing Koalas in New South Wales. Sydney, New South Wales National Parks and Wildlife Service, 1990, pp. 9-31.

SMITH, P. 'The Impact of Urbanisation on Wildlife Habitat with Reference to the Koala: Suggestions for Planning and Management', In Brown, R.A. ed. *Planning for Wildlife (Koala) Habitat Protection: Proceedings Workshop 89*. The University of Queensland and The Australian Koala Foundation, 1989, pp. 27-38.

SMITH, P. and SMITH, J. 'Warringah Shire Koala Study'. Prepared for the Warringah Shire Council, 1989.

STARR, J. 'Management of Koalas in an Urban Environment', In Lee, A.K.; Handasyde, K.A. and Sanson, G.D. eds. *Biology of the Koala*. New South Wales, Surrey Beatty & Sons, 1991, pp. 55-74.

STARR, J.; MORAN, E. and WHITEHOUSE, D. 'The Port Macquarie Experience', In Lunney, D.; Urquhart, C.A. and Reed, P. eds. *Proceedings of the Koala Summit on Managing Koalas in New South Wales*. Sydney, New South Wales National Parks and Wildlife Service, 1990, pp. 67-68.

STRAHAN, R. ed. *The Australian Museum Complete Book of Australian Mammals*. Sydney, Angus & Robertson Publishers, 1983.

SUMMERVILLE, K. 'Koalas in the Tweed Shire', In Lunney, D. Urquhart, C.A. and Reed, P. eds. *Proceedings of the Koala Summit on Managing Koalas in New South Wales*. Sydney, New South Wales National Parks and Wildlife Service, 1990, pp. 74-76.

SUZUKI, D. *Time to Change*. Toronto, Stoddart Publishing, 1993.

VICKERS-RICH, P.; RICH, T. *Wildlife of Gondwana*. Sydney, Reed Books, 1993.

WALL, D. *The Complete Adventures of Blinky Bill*. Australia, Angus & Robertson Publishers, 1939.

WHITE, M.E. *After the Greening: The Browning of Australia*. Kenthurst, Sydney, Kangaroo Press, 1994.

WHITE, N.A. and KUNST, N.D. 'Aspects of the Ecology of the Koala in Southeastern Queensland', In Lee, A.K.; Handasyde, K.A. and Sanson, G.D. eds. *Biology of the Koala*. New South Wales, Surrey Beatty & Sons, 1991, pp. 55-74.

WILMER, J.M.W.; MELZER, A.; CARRICK, F.; MORITZ, C. 'Low Genetic Diversity and Inbreeding Depression in Queensland Koalas', In *Wildlife Research* Vol. 20 (2), pp. 177-188.

WINGROVE, K. ed. *Norman Lindsay's Bears*. Melbourne, The Macmillan Company of Australia, 1978.

Picture Credits

The publisher and author wish to thank the following photographers and illustrators for the use of their photographs and illustrations. The letters after the page numbers indicate the illustration position, e.g., *b bottom, t top, l left, r right, c centre, m middle*.

Australian Koala Foundation 19b, maps on page 61c&r
Australian Land Survey and Information Group The maps on page 62 are © Commonwealth Copyright, AUSLIG, Australia's national mapping agency. They have been reproduced with the permission of the General Manager, Australian Surveying and Land Information Group, Department of Administrative Services, Canberra, ACT.
Wendy Blanshard 68, 69l, 69r, 70tl, 70r, 71
T. Dick © **Australian Museum** 100l, 100r, 103
John Garnsworthy & Associates Maps on pages 15 and 53 are artistic interpretations by John Garnsworthy & Associates of maps in *Koalas: The little Australians we'd all hate to lose*, by Bill Phillips. The illustrations and artwork on pages 24, 84, 86, 87 and 117b are also by John Garnsworthy & Associates.
Ron Garrison 13, 16tr, 20ml, 20mc, 23tl, 25t, 37r, 55, 73, 77tr, 77b, 92, 93, 108, 135, 141, 156
Georgeanne Irvine 12, 94l, 120, 149
John Oxley Library, Queensland 105
Kookaburra Productions cartoons on pages 61 and 114 courtesy of Kookaburra Productions
Norman Lindsay © **Janet Glad** illustration on pages 126-127, 153
Dick Marks 109
Mitchell State Library of New South Wales 104
Kevin Murphy 43r
National Library of Canberra 51
Nature Focus © 101
Steven Phillips 115, 117t, 123
Christiane Scheffler 16br, 19t, 22, 34-35, 38, 39, 44, 45, 48, 50, 52, 60r, 63l, 63r, 67, 79l, 79r, 83, 88, 89, 98, 99, 107t, 107br, 113, 118, 119, 124, 125, 128t, 129, 130, 131, 133tl, 133bl, 133r, 142, 143t, 143b, 150t, 150c, 150b, 151t, 151b, 152
Ann Sharp 80, 148r
Peter Solness 97
Dorothy Wall 128b
Philip Wright front cover, 2-3, 4-5, 6-7, 9, 10-11, 14-15, 16l, 17, 18, 20t, 20mr, 20b, 21, 23tr, 23bl, 23br, 25b, 26-27, 28, 29, 30, 31l, 31tr, 31br, 32t, 32b, 33t, 33b, 36, 37l, 40, 41, 42, 43l, 47, 49, 54, 56-7, 58l, 58r, 59, 60l, 64-65, 66, 72, 75, 76, 77tl, 78, 81, 82, 91, 94r, 95, 107bl, 110-111, 112, 122, 127, 134, 136-137, 138, 139, 140l, 140r, 144, 146, 147, 148l, 154-155

Index

Aboriginal peoples 18, 22, 50, 83, 99-104, 105
albinism 76-77
alpha (dominant) males 34, 68, 74, 84-85, 89
anthropomorphisation 129
Australian Koala Foundation 52, 53, 63, 116, 120-121
    139-141
Avalon 120

bellowing 46, 96
birth 68-69
Blinky Bill 126, 128, 129, 131
body size 34
brain 32
breeding season 67, 68
Brisbane 24-25, 53
Bunyip Bluegum 126, 129
bushfire 51, 55, 76, 104, 116-117, 121

caecum 37, 38, 69
camouflage 30-31
captivity 57, 58, 67, 96, 106, 108
carer groups 141-142
carrying capacity 56, 119
chlamydia 55, 56, 68, 78, 108
claws 31, 42
climate adaptation 29, 46
climbing 42
cloaca 69, 70
coastal land 121
communication 46, 83
community groups 142
conservation 14, 58, 115, 121, 130-132, 134, 139,
    145-149
corridor 87, 93-94
Cotts Harbour 118

decline 93, 114, 119-122, 149
development 113, 116, 121, 153
diastema 37
diet 34, 35, 38
digestion 34, 35, 37-38
Diprotodonta 17
disease 51, 68, 73, 78, 114
dispersal 56, 68, 70, 71, 73, 87, 89-90
distribution 24, 48-65
    New South Wales 54-55
    Queensland 53-54
    South Australia 57
    Victoria 55-57
dogs 33, 79, 92, 114, 116, 118, 153
Dreaming, The 18, 22, 103-104
drought 22, 38, 51, 76, 104, 114

ears 31, 32, 33
eco-tourism 132
education 130-131, 145-146
energy requirements 34
Eucalyptus 18, 31, 34, 35, 38, 60, 70
extinction 63, 93, 116, 120
eyes 33

faecal pellets 38
fecundity 56, 73
folivore 18
fossils 15, 17, 18
foxes 79
fragmentation 116-117
French Island 54, 55
fur 30-31, 34, 43, 45, 46, 100
fur trade 46, 51, 101, 104, 105-106, 128

gait 42
genetic diversity 52, 90
Gondwana 14, 15
government agencies 142
grooming 42, 45

habitat 51, 60-63, 106, 119, 120, 140, 142
habitat fragmentation 52
habitat protection 61, 140
heat regulation 45
hierarchy 74, 83, 84-85, 92, 96
home range 33, 60, 83, 85-89, 95
hunting 50-51, 101, 106

icon 13, 125
incisors 17
isolation 13, 14, 15

juveniles 71
    dispersal of 71-72, 89-90

Kangaroo Island 55, 57
Kenny Koala 129
Koala Habitat Atlas 52, 61, 63, 140, 148
Koala Park 108

lactation 69
legend 102-103
legislation 106, 115, 116, 140, 144, 148, 149, 153
life expectancy 74-76
Lismore 90, 118
Litokoala 17
Lone Pine Koala Sanctuary 74

macropods 17
Madakoala 17
mammals 16, 35, 38
management 92, 95-96
marsupials 14, 15, 16, 22, 29, 34, 38
mating 67, 68, 74, 88
Mesozoic era 14
metabolic rate 31, 34
milk 70
monotremes 16
motor vehicles 79, 92, 113, 114, 116

National Parks 121
National Parks and Wildlife Service 122, 142
Nature Conservation Act 1992 116
nesting hollows 24
New South Wales 54-55, 105, 118, 121
Norman Lindsay 126, 129, 153
nose 29, 31, 32, 33

oestrous 33, 67, 68, 73, 74
old age 79
old growth forests 22, 24, 55, 114, 121
overpopulation 56, 118

Pangaea 14
pap 69, 70
paws 31, 42
Perikoala 17
Phascolarctidae 17
Phascolarctos cinereus 18, 22
phenolics 35
Phillip Island 55
Pittwater 43
placentals 15, 16
play 17, 96
Polyprotodonta 17
population 53, 114
    captive 57-58
Port Macquarie 118
pouch 16, 33, 69, 70, 71
predators 76
pregnancy 68-69

Queensland 53-54, 105-106, 116-118, 122

rainforest 18
Raymond Island 55, 56
rehabilitation 142
research 140, 142, 143, 145
roads 79, 86, 93, 94, 113

San Diego Zoo 148
sanctuaries 31, 57, 58, 106-108, 132, 145
scent gland 32-33, 88
Scotland Island 43
scrotum 33
sexual maturity 33, 34, 73, 74

size 34
sleep 43, 45
social organisation 83, 84-92
South Australia 57, 105, 119
sperm 74
state-owned land 121
stress 78-79
swimming 42-43, 85
Sydney 54
symbols of koala 125-126, 130, 134

tail 22, 31, 38
teat 69, 70
tectonic plates 14
teeth 17, 37, 79
territoriality 33, 96
The Magic Pudding 126, 129
threats, man-made 79
    dogs 79
    foxes 79
    logging 22-24
    roads 79
threats, natural 76-79
    bushfire 76
    disease 77
    drought 76
    stress 78-79
thumbs 42
ticks 42
tourism 109, 126, 132-134
Tower Hill, Victoria 122
transients 89
translocation 56
Tucki Tucki 90-92
tunnels 94, 118
twins 68

Uncle Wattleberry 126
urbanisation 93, 114, 115, 116, 122

vegetation, 1788 62
    present 62
Victoria 55-57, 105, 118-119
vocalisation 46
Vombatoidea 17

weight 34
Westerport Bay 55
white settlement 51, 100-101
wildlife corridor 87, 93-94
wombats 16, 17, 70, 74

zoos 31